"As I read *Music for the Soul, Healing for the Heart*, I found myself being pulled through each page until I reached the end. I could not put it down. With each chapter, I sensed God's presence speaking into my heart as I experienced the stories and testimonies behind Steve's journey. This book impacted my heart in a deep and real way and is truly a labor of love that points to God and His faithfulness and provision to bring comfort, hope, peace, and healing. God uses music to touch our souls. This book will inspire you, bring you to tears, and encourage you in your journey."

Joseph Northcut, Director of Church Ministries
ChurchInitiative.org

"An insightful, liberating, and heartwarming story of how God can take an average guy and turn him into a psalmist of healing. *Music for the Soul, Healing for the Heart* reaches the pain that touches us all and gives wings to our crippled soul. Finally, we are free to soar with the Song of the Lord written just for our life."

Dawn Damon, Pastor
Tribes Church, Grand Rapids, Michigan
Author of *When a Woman You Love Was Abused*

"Music for the Soul touches our souls by writing and singing songs that matter. They are committed to making music that dares to step up to the plate right when others walk away or don't know what to do. They take on the hard problems of life in an ever-redemptive way. I would recommend that not only individuals but churches, counseling centers, Christian colleges, and recovery centers keep a supply of these music collections on hand to give when they desperately need something to hand to a friend."

Gloria Gaither, Grammy and Dove Award-winning Songwriter, Author, and Speaker

"C. S. Lewis, once said, 'Pain insists upon being attended to.' Steve Siler beautifully captures stories that speak to emptiness, abuse, grief and loss, depression and suicide, addiction, and the sanctity of life. As someone who has lived and worked in the mental health field for over thirty-five years, I am confident that *Music for the Soul, Healing for the Heart* will both impact and transform the lives of many who are hurting and broken."

Eric Scalise, PhD, LPC, LMFT
Former Vice President, American Association of Christian Counselors; President, LIV Enterprises & Consulting, LLC

"Steve Siler's story makes a compelling case for continuing to move forward in the pursuit of God's call on one's life, even when you find yourself in the crosshairs of opposition. A truly inspiring read!"

Constance Rhodes, Founder and CEO, FINDINGbalance, Inc.
Author, *Life Inside the "Thin" Cage*

"David put all of his heart's questions and cries and exultation of God into his songs. Those Psalms still move and motivate us today, as God hoped they would. And I add Steve Siler's heartfelt songs to that list. I know God does too."

Pat Boone, Singer, Actor, Author, Songwriter

"A terrific story of brokenness and the way God soothes human pain with a song. Compelling, it sings hope with every story. *You* know someone who needs to hear the encouraging notes that God loves him, God hears her pain, and God sings over them with the comfort of a new song. Read and share this book!"

Marnie C. Ferree, MA, LMFT
Director of Bethesda Workshops, Nashville, Tennessee
Author of *No Stones*

"Through the years our clients have been greatly blessed by the healing music of Music for the Soul. As you discover the powerful stories behind this fantastic ministry, you too will be blessed!"

Gregory L. Jantz, PhD, CEDS
Founder, The Center • A Place of HOPE
Author of *Hope and Healing from Emotional Abuse*

MUSIC
FOR THE SOUL
HEALING
FOR THE HEART

lessons from a life in song

STEVE SILER

Cover Design: Yvonne Parks
Music for the Soul Logo: Linda Crossan
Interior Design/Typesetting: Lisa Parnell

ISBN: 978-1-942306-49-8 (Print)
ISBN: 978-1-942306-50-4 (eBook)

Printed in the United States of America

23 22 21 20 19 18 17 16   1 2 3 4 5

FOR MEREDITH, STEPHANIE, AND HENRY—
the music of my soul

CONTENTS

FOREWORD

Have you ever met someone who you instantly knew would change peoples' lives? Like a great inventor, you sensed he was on to something profound. That's what happened to me when I first met Steve Siler and listened to his story. I was fascinated to know how a music writer and producer could use his creative gift to touch the heart of so many people in such a unique way.

I knew God was up to something new with Steve. Despite his success in the secular music world, he was restless. He wanted to use his powerful medium of music to do more than entertain. While entertainment is fine, Steve wanted to be part of something with eternal significance. Music, he believed, could reach people in a way that spoken words could not. Music touches the innermost parts of us.

Steve knew that lyrics capture the heart and that a melodic line can become deeply ingrained in the brain. We frail humans are hardwired to respond to music as it stimulates more parts of the brain than we can imagine. Music changes the brain and has a profound power on our emotions. It arouses feelings, reaches into our memories, and unites us.

As I read the lyrics to the Music for the Soul songs, I hear echoes of sentiments expressed by so many of my former patients, my friends, and my family. Then I listen to those words put to melodies that are both haunting and hopeful. Music for the Soul is a musical journey through the stories of our lives—stories we can all relate to through our experiences, as well as the experiences of those we care about so deeply.

As a therapist who has been in clinical practice for more than twenty years, I am familiar with emotional pain. Like you, I've had my own issues to work through—a brother killed by terrorism, a mom with cancer, infertility, and more. Emotional pain is inescapable in this life, but thankfully, healing is not. And music can be a vital component of that healing.

Steve took our struggles and put them to music in a way that has the power to move and change us. His musical journey often frees us to feel things locked deeply in our hearts. Each story he shares brings hope and heart transformation and reminds us that we are not alone in this journey called life.

I am so thankful that Steve found a way to harness the power of healing music through his God-given talents. His passion for this work and personal sacrifice to make Music for the Soul a reality are evident when you read his story. God shifted his priorities and birthed a ministry that has helped many people, often in miraculous and life-changing ways.

Music for the Soul, Healing for the Heart is a reminder of how God uses our talents to further His work when we are willing to surrender to His plan. Be encouraged through Steve's story. You may be used by God in ways you never imagined.

Music for the Soul is a melody of hope, offering balm for weary travelers and rest for our often-troubled souls. Enjoy the ride and share this message of hope with those around you.

Linda Mintle, PhD
February 2016

PREFACE

I remember it like it was yesterday. I'm in the middle of a large crowd at a Christian concert in Nashville, Tennessee. All evening long the duo on stage has been singing songs from their new CD. The audience has been listening in appreciation. But now the artists have invited everybody to sing along as they begin a well-known song.

Almost immediately audience members are on their feet and singing. At first I'm singing too, but it isn't long before I'm struggling to get the words out. The next thing I know I'm having trouble standing. I can't see through the tears, and my body feels weak. The song is about the love of Jesus. The words are saying that I'm forgiven. The melody is saying it too.

How can this be? I've betrayed someone who trusted me. What I've done was so, so selfish, and I'm deeply ashamed. It *feels* unforgiveable.

But the mercy will not be denied. It's as if I have been hit in the back of the head with a board. This is no tender mercy. This is a hammer of grace. And it is being delivered on the wings of a powerful melody and a lyric.

People have spoken words just like the words in this song to me before, but I was always able to rationalize them away. Tonight, however, there is no defense against this music. God has used the combined power of the melody and lyric not just to create a thin place but to totally break through.

I've experienced an ambush. My heart is defenseless. Before I know it I have been driven to my knees, sobbing uncontrollably in a public place. The friend who has come with me doesn't know what is happening. But I do—even though I can't speak. And in that moment I am healed of my shame. I will never be the same.

Simultaneously stirring and sublime, God's gift of song can permeate our soul at its deepest level. A song can often articulate our story better than we can ourselves, in a life-giving language that restores our hope.

Over the past thirty years of writing and producing music, I've watched songs melt walls of defense time and again. I've seen songs create profound moments of emotional release, freeing people from pain they have long hidden deeply in their hearts.

That's what this book is about. It's about miraculous encounters with the Creator of the universe. It's about how God's hand is at work in music and in our lives—moving us, transforming us, and, ultimately, even healing us.

My prayer is that some of these stories will speak the truth of your heart. May God bless you with songs that sing the music of *your* soul.

ROAD TO A PRAYER

"Music, the greatest good that mortals know,
and all of heaven we have below."
JOSEPH ADDISON

"Ladies and Gentlemen, the Beatles!" With those words and a wave of his hand—not to mention a cascade of frenzied screams—Ed Sullivan introduced the Fab Four to American television audiences on his iconic Sunday evening variety show. It was February 9, 1964.[*]

My whole life changed that night, which makes me about as unique as a grain of sand on the beach. Millions of lives were changed that night, and the face of popular music, not only in the United States but also throughout the entire world, was never the same.

I can't even imagine how many parents purchased guitars for pleading children in the weeks following that performance. I only know that one of them showed up at my house.

To begin with, I wanted a drum kit. But after more thought, I decided that because Ringo sat in the back, I would rather have a guitar so I could be out in front and get more attention. Obviously,

---

[*] An invitation to be on *The Ed Sullivan Show* was the stamp of approval for entertainers in the 1960s.

1

I was not yet familiar with the concept in Matthew 20:16, that the first shall be last and the last shall be first!

So it was that on a whim, and thanks to the British rock and roll invasion, my journey to a Christian music songwriting career began.

My parents were Sunday school teachers in Kokomo, Indiana, when I was a toddler; but by the time the Beatles burst on the scene, we were living in southern California, and my folks were not attending church. Still, my mom, Carole, did speak of God often and the importance of her faith. She sang solos in church during the years they lived in Indiana, and the standard rendition of "The Lord's Prayer" was one of her favorites. Prayer before meals was a regular part of our daily routine—"Lord, bless this food to our use and us to Thy service."

I only have one memory of attending church as a small child. I asked my dad to take me to an Easter Service at a little wooden church about a mile from our house in the San Fernando Valley, a suburb of Los Angeles. Little did I know that not quite twenty years later I would be married at that same Little Brown Church in the Valley and that it would be there that I played my first Christian song in public and where the genesis of my ministry would take place.

It wasn't until I was sixteen that I began to attend church regularly. I suppose my reason for finally attending church was about as original as my reason for becoming interested in music. A beautiful young lady with long blonde hair—thirty-one inches to be exact—invited me.

Going to School

Thanks to Robin Perna I met Jesus Christ that summer at the First Baptist Church of Sherman Oaks, and within a year I wrote my first Christian song, entitled "There Is No Greater Love." That, of course, is true, but there are many thousands of greater *songs*. However, it was a hint of things to come.

From the very first time I picked up the guitar, I had been drawn to songwriting.

My parents encouraged me in the kinds of ways I wish that all children could be encouraged. My mom came up with harmony parts for all of my songs, and we sang them together while my dad beamed and recorded them on a reel-to-reel tape recorder.

The lyrics were what you would expect from a ten-year-old. "Fisherman, the shark just ate up Dan," "I've got a hole in my pants and in are crawling the ants," and so on. Even at that, my parents never laughed at me. In retrospect I have no idea how they pulled that off!

> From the very first time I picked up the guitar, I had been drawn to songwriting.

But here's the thing. Listening back to those songs many years later, I could hear that the gift of melody writing was already there, God given. Yes, I had been devouring songs as a listener—I must have listened to the *Mary Poppins* soundtrack five hundred times!— but lots of kids love listening to music and never become melody writers. I was blessed to have been given a knack for putting notes together in a way that made people want to sing.

The encouragement of my parents continued throughout middle school and high school, sometimes to an unreasonable degree. One time my dad, Russ, borrowed a friend's pickup truck and moved our piano to someone else's house so that my band could play a birthday party gig for which we were paid a whopping sixteen dollars! What makes this story even more remarkable is that I didn't even play the piano at the time. I was the *guitar* player!

As the years passed, they were filled with guitar lessons, piano lessons, and vocal lessons. In middle school, which we called junior high, I played double bass in the school orchestra, trombone in the school band, and guitar in the jazz ensemble.

I remember a battle of the bands where there were four bands and I was in three of them. And I *still* lost! All of the bands I was in played original songs. By now the lyrics were more sophisticated, but there was no way we were going to beat the guys who knew how to play "Smoke on the Water" by Deep Purple!

Undeterred, I kept writing originals, many of them with my friend Sean Sutton. It was our goal to be the Lennon and McCartney songwriting team of our school, and we put together a band with the impossibly pretentious name the Vehicle of Aestheticism. (Of course on the bass drum head we shortened it to VOA since no one knew what it meant anyway.) By the time we were in ninth grade, we had written more than two hundred songs together. In effect, we were "going to school" while we were going to school.

Will It Fly?

In high school my focus on music became even more extreme. I had the good fortune to attend Grant High School in Van Nuys at a time when the music program was one of the best in all of the Los Angeles area, and quite possibly one of the best in the country.

Again, I played double bass in the orchestra. I also joined the choir. Our choir teacher, Francis Norbert, was a singer in the Roger Wagner Master Chorale, one of the preeminent vocal groups in southern California.

Both Mrs. Norbert and the orchestra teacher, Miles Neil, challenged us with material suited to adults. Several members of this orchestra went on to professional music careers as classical musicians in philharmonic orchestras around the world. Of the seven bass players in the bass section, five went on to play music professionally. I can still remember the chill that ran up and down my spine when our bass section laid the foundation for Samuel Barber's "Adagio for Strings" with the violins soaring high and ever higher above us. Experiencing the music from the inside out, as part of the larger group, was a thrilling experience.

Popular forms of music were also well represented at our high school. Several members of the rock band Toto, later known for hits like "Africa" and "Rosanna," were regular performers at our school dances.

Anyone who has ever participated in an orchestra, a choir, a marching band, a jazz ensemble, a bluegrass band, or a rock group knows the thrill of being *inside* the music. Beyond the sound and the emotional tone of the music itself, the communication and teamwork that takes place when one is creating music with others is exhilarating!

God is not a wasteful God.

After high school came a period that can perhaps best be described as wandering in the desert. God is not a wasteful God, and I believe that everything that happened was preparation for what was to come. The path, however, seems a study in circumlocution and is certainly not a plan that anyone but a very creative God could have ever drawn up!

It all began with my mom reaching out to an old friend on my behalf. When our family first moved to southern California, we landed in a little apartment on Gardner Street in Hollywood. From there my mom went looking for a job, and she found one a few miles away at United Western Recorders on Sunset Boulevard.

At that time United Western was one of the favorite recording studios of people like Frank Sinatra and Ella Fitzgerald, so my mom wound up meeting a lot of talented people. One of the people she befriended was a young recording engineer named Bones Howe, who later went on to produce numerous iconic hits for groups such as the Association, the Turtles, and the Fifth Dimension.

So my mom, having decided that I was ready for some mentoring as a writer and potential recording artist, called up her old friend Bones and asked if he would see me.

Over the next couple of years Bones coached me on my song-writing and allowed me to spend time with him in the studio watching recording sessions. I remember one time he walked in and saw me studying a large recording console. "What do you think, Steve? Will it fly?" he quipped.

Bones made one of my lifetime dreams come true by inviting me to the studio one afternoon to meet his friend Paul McCartney who was recording the *Venus and Mars* album at Wally Heider Studios in Hollywood. "Spirits of Ancient Egypt" was pumping out of the overhead speakers when we entered the studio. I can't remember where I put my keys this morning, but I can remember every detail of what Paul was wearing that day, from his black vest and long-sleeved white shirt rolled up to the elbows down to his black sandals. His wife, Linda, was seated at his left, eating cole slaw from a deli tin.

Shortly thereafter, I put together a band for a showcase at the famous Troubadour club in West Hollywood. Afterward Bones responded very positively, leading me to believe that before long he would be bringing me into the studio to record some songs. Over the next several months, however, it became clear that he had cooled on the idea. At the time it was bitterly disappointing.

Still, I will always be grateful to Bones for making time for a green kid to hang out and absorb some of what the real music industry was like.

During the next fifteen years I had a dizzying array of diverse musical experiences:

- Performing as a solo artist at a variety of Los Angeles music clubs. Thanks to my friend Rich Sperber, who ushered at the Hollywood Bowl, I even got to play there twice!
- Writing the music scores to three short films made by my friends Michael Johnson and Adam Greenman, both of whom went on to successful movie industry careers.

- Working at A&M Records as part of the promotion team for artists like the Police ("Roxanne"), Styx ("Come Sail Away"), Gino Vannelli ("I Just Wanna Stop"), and Chuck Mangione ("Feels So Good").
- Putting together a Top Forty band called "Livacious" (ya know—live and vivacious) and touring Sheraton and Holiday Inn lounges from coast to coast playing songs like "The Girl from Ipanema," "Maneater," and "Funkytown."
- Purchasing a disco ball and putting together a DJ business called "Rug Cutters." (It's a slang term for dancing that emerged during the 1920s. I know, you're thinking, *What's with this guy and all the weird names?*) I presided over hundreds of first dances at weddings and called Bingo at more than my share of corporate picnics.

Then finally one day the long-suffering woman I had been dating for several years, who thankfully would later agree to become my wife in spite of all of the above, asked me rather pointedly, "Do you plan to make a living at this songwriting thing anytime soon, or is it just a hobby?"

Ouch!

A Long and Fascinating Detour

It was from that day forward that I decided to treat songwriting like a job instead of a glorified hobby. This meant taking classes on songwriting and studying great songs to see what made them great. Most importantly, it meant creating a regular writing schedule of several hours a week and sticking to it even though I had a full-time job. God bless the neighbors in my apartment building who endured my banging away on the piano every night with uncommon good grace. Eviction would have been totally reasonable.

Finally, it meant being willing to put myself out there—taking every meeting I could get, playing my songs for publishers and managers.

Eventually—after countless rejections and several agonizingly close calls—treating songwriting like a job paid off, and I signed my first single song contract with a publishing company called Catdaddy Music. The song was called "Lovers Can Make Anything Happen." Otis Williams of the Temptations produced a version of the song for an artist named Tony Warren, but Tony was never signed and the song was never released.

> I was not yet plowing in the field that God had prepared for me.

A few months after signing the song with Catdaddy, I co-wrote a song with Catdaddy's owner Tena Clark. That song resulted in my second single song contract and the first time something I had written was recorded and appeared on an album!

This was my first lesson in not being able to control where your songs wind up or how they are used. The tune was an innocuous break-up song called "I'm Gonna Make It Easy." The premise was, "If you're going to keep mistreating me, I'm going to leave you." Certainly not the most important song ever written, but it was harmless enough.

So, imagine my dismay when I opened up the record jacket and realized the Amsterdam-based group the Dolly Dots, who had recorded the song, had posed in a, shall we say, somewhat compromising manner for one of the album photos. This was not an album I would be showing to my mom and dad.

Undaunted, however, I carried on. It would take two more experiences like that for me to get the message that I was not yet plowing in the field that God had prepared for me.

The first of these experiences took shape after a long and fascinating detour.

Growing up in Los Angeles I'd always been a big Dodgers

baseball fan and spent hundreds of summer hours listening to the iconic baseball announcer Vin Scully. So when my friend Rich Sperber, also a huge Dodgers fan, suggested that we write a song to honor Scully, I jumped at the chance.

Rich had learned that Scully's wife had several members of her family who were affected by a rare degenerative eye disease called retinitis pigmentosa. Tragically, the disease often eventually results in blindness. He suggested we write the song about Scully and offer to donate a large portion of any proceeds to RP International.

It just so happened that Rich was able to do a virtually spot-on impression of Vin Scully!

We wrote and recorded the song, "Vinny Is the Voice," complete with sound effects of a cheering ballpark crowd and some exciting Scully voice-overs by Rich. Peter O' Malley, the president of the Dodgers at the time, loved it, and Helen Harris, the founder and president of RP International, loved it as well.

The only person who didn't love it was Vin Scully.

We were crushed. But rather than let things stall there, Rich and I decided to meet with Harris and propose writing a theme song for her organization. She loved the idea. Little did we know we were opening the proverbial can of worms.

There had recently been this little song called "We Are the World" recorded by Michael Jackson, Lionel Richie, Bruce Springsteen, Diana Ross, Billy Joel, Ray Charles, and several other megastars as a fund-raiser for African hunger relief.

Helen's idea was to take the song we had written for her, entitled "Forgotten Eyes," and take a "We Are the World" approach to recording it. She also took a the-more-the-merrier approach to inviting people to be involved.

That's how we wound up with a final recording with a cast of literally hundreds that included comedian Bob Hope (in his eighties at the time), Smokey Robinson, Sammy Davis Jr. (his last recording), Patti LaBelle, Mel Tormé, fifties teen idol Connie

Francis, Andrae Crouch (my first brush with Christian music!), Jack Jones (of *The Love Boat* theme fame), Dionne Warwick, Cheryl Ladd (from the *Charlie's Angels* TV show), jazz piano legend Herbie Hancock, Sister Sledge, and George Burns (the cigar-chomping comedian who actually played God in a movie).

Entertainment Tonight showed up at the initial vocal recording session at Evergreen Recording Studios in Burbank, California. Several more recording sessions followed, eventually resulting in over one hundred tracks of vocals. Producer Lee Holdridge did his best to create a serviceable final version from this widely disparate collection of celebrities, but the song eventually collapsed from the weight of an identity crisis and the recording's being an obvious attempt to repeat the We-Are-the-World formula.

The song, however, was definitely an early indicator of the ministry that was to come:

> *Remember the green of the grass in the springtime*
> *Remember the gold autumn leaves on the ground*
> *You don't have to remember 'cause the seasons return*
> *and you'll see them the next time around*
>
> *But what of the child with sight quickly fading*
> *The next flower she sees just might be her last*
> *Will she have to imagine the blue daylight sky*
> *Through a nighttime that never will pass*
>
> *For the children*
> *For the eyes of tomorrow*
> *We can light the darkness*
> *We can end the sorrow*
> *For the children*
> *In our hands their future lies*
> *Together we will never let there be forgotten eyes*[1]

Patti LaBelle, one of the bigger names Harris secured for the "Forgotten Eyes" recording, had not been able to join everyone for the big session at Evergreen so I was dispatched to Philadelphia.

I took a red-eye, leaving Los Angeles International Airport at midnight with a reel of heavy two-inch recording tape under my arm. When I arrived in Philadelphia, I washed my hair in the airport bathroom and stuck my head underneath the hand dryer. Sleep deprived, I decided to take a cab to the studio rather than renting a car.

When I got there I remember the studio engineer telling me excitedly, "Some of the Eagles were here yesterday!" Naturally my mind went to the music group. Glenn Frey? Don Henley?

I had forgotten where I was. It took me a minute to realize he was talking about the *Philadelphia* Eagles, the NFL team. The studio had been full of football players!

Patti LaBelle was a total pro, and once I got my bearings, the session went great. When we were done I stuck around for awhile and wound up meeting two very successful songwriters who were there working with LaBelle on her new album.

It turned out that one of the writers lived only a few minutes from me in southern California. I asked for his phone number, which he gave me.

I can still remember how nervous I was, days later, making that call. This was someone who was having big hits as a songwriter. He had the life I wanted. My fears were unwarranted. We set up a meeting. When we got together he was very kind and encouraging to me. We hit it off and wound up collaborating. Before long we'd written several very good songs but as time passed, though we had some close calls, none of them were getting picked up by recording artists.

I was becoming desperate to make a living as a songwriter. I just wanted to get paid to write something. About that time my co-writer was offered the opportunity to write a theme song for the opening of a new Chippendale's exotic male dancing club in London. He asked me if I wanted to co-write it with him. I would receive $250 for my work on the song.

I said yes.

Is That All There Is?

The shame I felt in the wake of the decision to accept the Chippendale's assignment was a great and painful teacher. From that experience I learned that money alone was not going to bring me the satisfaction I was seeking as a songwriter, especially money earned at the expense of my values.

I've reflected many times over the years on the extreme grace of a God who would give the opportunity for a Christian music songwriting career and, ultimately, a ministry to a person who had so little faith as to sell out his belief system for $250. This grace was brought into even sharper relief later on when many of the ministry projects I was called to work on were to help those wounded by sexual objectification.

An important positive experience took place during that time frame. One of my friends from the high school bass section, Mike George, had gone on to play the electric bass professionally. While on a recording session he mentioned his "songwriter friend" to a television music supervisor named Lynne McCleery. Lynne was the Los Angeles representative for a New York-based company called Score Productions, which provided television music cues and theme songs for sports shows, soap operas, and game shows.

Lynne listened to my music, liked what she heard, and wound up giving me the opportunity to write for all different kinds of projects, gaining invaluable experience and some professional writing credits!

Without knowing it at the time, I was getting closer to being ready to hear what God had in mind for my music. The experience that finally tipped the scales came only a short while later.

I had written a pop dance tune with a couple of friends. This was soon after Paula Abdul's breakout success with the *Forever Your Girl* album. One of my friends had connections with a female Canadian pop singer who was looking to make the same kind of record. Our song basically replicated the formula of Abdul's hit single "Straight Up!"

Imagine how excited I was when I found out that our song was going to be the title track and the first single from Candi & the Backbeat's upcoming album *The World Just Keeps On Turning*. The anticipation of having a hit single was intoxicating! I remember the morning I drove over to the newsstand to get a copy of the new *Billboard* magazine. When I opened it up, there it was! A full-page, color ad trumpeting, "The new smash hit single!"

> I was getting closer to being ready to hear what God had in mind.

I remember thinking, *I'm on my way now!* The dream I had dreamed since I was a kid was about to come true!

A few days later I was in the living room of my apartment in Glendale, California, with the radio set to a station where I knew our song was on the playlist. I was so excited. All of a sudden, there it was! A song I had co-written was on the radio!

All the way back in 1969 crooner Peggy Lee, better known for her sultry hit "Fever," had a comeback hit with a song called "Is that All There Is?" It is a strange, maudlin song where the singer sees even the most standout events in her life as being disappointments.

After my song ended, I literally found myself thinking, *Is that all there is?*

Don't get me wrong. A big part of me was grateful. I had achieved a lifelong goal.

But as I listened I was struck by the forgettable-ness of the song. Oh, it was "hooky" enough and easy to sing along with, but it wasn't going to make a meaningful difference in anyone's life, including mine. It wasn't that it was amoral or anything like that. I already had learned that lesson. It was just that it was disposable, a piece of ear candy. There was nothing of real value in it. There was nothing of *me* in it. And there was certainly nothing eternal about it. It would be here today and gone tomorrow.

I couldn't believe it. Had I worked all those years for *this*? Instead of the absolute elation I had expected to feel, I felt a nagging sense of disappointment.

By this time my wife and I were regularly attending that little brown church in which we were married. Though being located in the crowded San Fernando Valley, the church had, since opening in 1945, kept its doors "locked" open twenty-four hours a day. A humble wooden building, with grass growing in between the planks of the walls, it became a beacon in the night for many in the southern California community. It was truly a sanctuary and the perfect place to go and sit with one's questions.

So it was that I went to the church in the middle of the night and sat quietly by myself for a long, long time. Then I had a one-way conversation with God. "Lord, I know that You gave me this gift of music. And now I know that I'm not doing what You want me to be doing with it. Please show me how to make a difference with my music. And if I'm not supposed to being doing music at all, then show me what I am supposed to be doing. I just want to be doing something that matters."

I was thirty-four years old and had been a Christian for eighteen years. And for the *first time ever* I was finally asking God what I should be doing with my life.*

---

* Whenever I speak to college students now, I routinely recommend that they consider asking that question *first*!

Now I was ready to learn about a deeper purpose for music and songwriting than I had ever thought possible.

THE SOUNDTRACK OF OUR LIVES

"Music is a moral law. It gives soul to the universe,
wings to the mind, flight to the imagination, a charm to sadness,
gaiety and life to everything. It is the essence of order
and lends to all that is good, just, and beautiful."
PLATO

Have you ever thought about how ubiquitous music is in our culture? It's everywhere! It is woven into the very fabric of our lives.

Community, the framework through which we live out our faith, is reinforced by music. Whether it is "Open the Eyes of My Heart" or "Amazing Grace," we always have music when we gather in our churches—even if the style may vary from steeple to steeple. But it's not just at church. For example, generations of Americans have played music at county fairs and community barn dances. We've sung songs around campfires. We, or our kids, have participated in school musicals.

Every college has an alma mater and a rousing "fight song." Every outdoor college or professional sporting event in the US starts with the national anthem. "We Will Rock You" routinely rings out from stadium speakers. "Take Me Out to the Ballgame" is part of the seventh inning stretch at every baseball game.

And whether it's "Happy Birthday to You," "Pomp and Circumstance," or "Here Comes the Bride," music is always an important part of the major life events we share with those dearest to us.

God has given us music as a way to swiftly access and engage our emotions.

Filmmakers know this. Why do you squirm in your seat when a woman is walking down a dark hallway on the screen? Because the music is telling you something scary is about to happen! Why do grown men sob at the end of *Field of Dreams* when Kevin Costner is having a catch with his dad? Because the music is saying, "This is *sad*."

> Because it touches our emotions, music can inspire us to action.

Because it touches our emotions, music can inspire us to action. It has been the rallying cry for protest movements for years, something that became particularly prominent with the advent of popular folk music in the fifties and grew in influence with the sixties and artists like Bob Dylan and Joan Baez. "We Shall Overcome" became a unifying anthem for the civil rights movement, so popular that President Lyndon Johnson invoked the song title in his state of the union address before the successful vote on the Civil Rights Act of 1964.

God has also wired our brains to respond to the *combination* of words and music. Advertisers have long known the memory power of songs. They've been singing to us about everything from beer to toilet bowl cleaner for years. Think about it. You can probably sing the jingles to five products right now without even trying that hard. And oh my goodness, they do stick with you. I can still sing the theme song Barry Manilow wrote for McDonald's back in the '70s whether I want to or not.

You deserve a break today
So get up and get away…

Music is piped into our shopping malls, our restaurants, our elevators, and even our dentist's offices. In a moment of sweet irony a few years ago I was treated to David Cook singing "Time of My Life" in the midst of having a root canal!

It Just Works

Music just works. It doesn't matter whether you want to inspire someone, get them revved up, make them sad, start their toe tapping, or lullaby them to sleep. Music works *every* time.

According to Daniel Levitin in his book *This Is Your Brain on Music*, the archaeological record shows an uninterrupted record of music making everywhere we find humans and in every era. "Music predates agriculture in the history of our species."[1]

I believe this speaks to something central that God has built into us as Creator—a deep appreciation and need for music.

While we subconsciously acknowledge the importance of music in our daily choices, we often don't consciously perceive the way music "feeds" us, impacting our spiritual, emotional, and even educational well-being. According to the American Music Conference, young people who are involved in making music in their teenage years score one hundred points higher on the SATs than those who don't play music. As clearly outlined above, music plays a central role in *every* area of our cultural life.

In music we have something that brings joy *and* comfort, something that speaks for us in ways that we can't always speak for ourselves. Music gives voice to the fullest possible range of human emotions. It sets free those things we can't hold inside any longer. It helps us fly. It helps us cry.

Music is the soundtrack of our lives.

When the towers came down in Manhattan, Karl Paulnack, a pianist and conservatory professor, found himself asking on September 12, 2001, "Who needs a piano player right now?"

Then, after several days of seeing the healing effect of music for the people of New York City, he came to understand that the musicians were not just entertainers but were "a lot closer to a paramedic, a firefighter, a rescue worker."[2]

Music was drawing the people together, telling their common story, and reminding them of their shared humanity at a time of unspeakable tragedy.

That is what music can do: it can help us *express the inexpressible*. Music is a gift from God, arguably the greatest gift of communication God has given to us. And when combined with language, as in the form of a song, it becomes a gift that is greater than the sum of its parts. It helps us tell—and understand—our own stories.

Something Important

I began to understand the true power of music for the first time when I stopped focusing on trying to become the next Peter Frampton (younger readers, think John Mayer) and started trying to think about how God wanted me to use my musical gifts.

After hearing my first song on the radio, I was pretty low. But even though God had been working on my heart for a long time, it was going to take something very specific to truly get my attention. It happened in a most unexpected way.

One day the phone rang, and it was a call from a man whom I had never met. It turns out that he had visited my church on the day when I played one of my Christian songs in the sanctuary for the first time ever.

He said, "My name is Stephen Breithaupt. I'm currently starring in *Les Misérables* at the Schubert Theater. I have licensed a Christian children's book on the issue of childhood sexual abuse, and I am going to produce a stage play with music. I think you're the guy who's supposed to write the songs."

This was it—an answer to my prayer to make a difference.

I went to meet with Stephen; and the minute he put the book on the table and I looked into the eyes of the child on the cover, I said, "I'll do it. I don't know if I'm qualified or not, but if you think I am, with God's help I'll try."

I went home that afternoon and read the book Stephen had given me. Then I got down on my knees next to the piano for the first time in my life. "Lord, I don't know why You have chosen me for this opportunity. But I know it is important. Please help me to write these songs."

> Music can help us express the inexpressible.

The book was *I Can't Talk about It* by Doris Sanford and Graci Evans.

It chronicled the story of a little girl who is being sexually abused by her father and how the spirit of God, appearing in the form of a dove, comes to her on the beach and helps her understand that she is not to blame for what is happening to her. The dove ultimately gives her the strength to speak out.

It was not until later that I remembered my mom had gone to the beach one day a few months earlier for a time of prayer. She was so troubled by my frustration over my music career that she devoted an entire day to praying about it. "I prayed so hard I left my body," she later told me. "When I got home, there was a dove sitting on our front porch. When I walked up to it, it didn't move. I knew then that God was answering my prayer and that I didn't need to worry about your career any longer."

Now here I was, writing songs from a book where the main character was named *Love Dove*!

After completing the songs, I took them to a therapist I knew on a Friday. I was concerned that what I'd written could potentially do more harm than good and wanted her honest opinion. "Would you listen to these and tell me if you think I've got anything here that would help somebody?"

The following Monday morning she called me. "Steve, I hope you won't be angry with me, but I used your songs with clients over the weekend."

That was an eye-opening moment for me! Here was a purpose for music that I'd never even considered.

The four songs I'd written based on *I Can't Talk about It* became the soundtrack for a play that Stephen and I would present dozens of time over the next three years—in churches, in theaters, at colleges, and even in the Los Angeles *public* elementary schools.

When I asked the women who invited us into the LA public school system, "Couldn't you get fired for letting us do such a blatantly Christian play in the schools?" she replied, "I don't care. It's the truth and the children need to see it." What made this even more remarkable was that she was Jewish. We wound up presenting the play for thousands of children across the Los Angles area, performing in twenty different communities in all.

In the years since, people have often said to me, "You could sell more copies of [this or that] project if you would just take Jesus out." I always remember my experience with the LA public schools. I learned then and there that I never need to apologize for, deny, or take Jesus out of a song to make someone comfortable. I create what I feel called to create, and then I knock on the doors and let God decide which ones to open.

After our experience in the schools, Stephen and I wanted to do an audio recording of the play complete with actors, singers, sound effects, and orchestration. The budget was going to be $25,000, and we had no idea how we would raise it.

One night we did a presentation of our musical play *I Can't Talk about It* at our own church. Ten people attended. We passed a hat after the performance. Among the scattered one-dollar and five-dollar bills, we found a check for two hundred dollars from

Don LaFontaine. Don's wife, Nita, had recorded a version of my song "Forgotten Eyes" five years earlier.

I followed up with Don to thank him. During that conversation I told him what we were hoping to accomplish. A few days later he invited me up to his home. When I walked in he asked me to sit down, and then he handed me a check for $20,000. I was stunned.

When I tried to thank him, he interrupted me and said, "No, Steve. Thank *you*. I've been very successful in my life, but I've never done anything that made a difference. You're giving me a chance to make a difference."*

Then he said something that I've returned to many times through the years of fundraising for Music for the Soul. "Never be afraid to ask for what you need in order to do what you do. The world needs what you do and you can't do it without support."

So it was that, with the help of Don, Nita, and others, I was able to go into the studio and, for the first time, record songs solely for the purpose of ministering to hurting people.

The responses we received to the recording were humbling and profound, and the comments I received about the songs were life changing for me.

"I used to take drugs every night to go to sleep. Now I listen to this," said one woman holding up the CD.

A therapist in Orange County, California, said to me, "I have a client who has been coming to me for two years and could not cry about her abuse. Then she heard your songs. Now she has opened up. The tears are flowing, and she is finally letting all of the pain out."

---

* Actually, Don LaFontaine was a very generous man and made a difference in many, many lives with his sense of humor, his willingness to mentor, and with both financial and in-kind donations to multiple organizations and individuals.

Because of a Song

Toward the end of the three years that Stephen and I worked together, an opportunity came to participate at VOICES, a conference for survivors of incest, in Newark, New Jersey. The directors of the conference had come across our recording of *I Can't Talk about It* and wanted us to perform the song "Innocent Child" from the project at the closing ceremonies of the conference. They were also offering us the opportunity to have a table at the conference where we would make the recording, and the book upon which it was based, available to the conference attendees.

> "The tears are flowing, and she is finally letting the pain out."

Unfortunately Breithaupt, who had performed the role of the dove on the project, was not available for the dates of the conference. But the opportunity seemed too important to pass up. So, although I considered myself only the composer and piano player and had never sung the song publicly before, I agreed to come and sing at the closing ceremony.

When I arrived at the conference, I found myself one of less than ten men at a gathering of more than three hundred people. The conference organizer approached and, cautioning me, said, "Don't hug these women. They hate to be hugged by men who are strangers." It made perfect sense, and as one who has always been a hugger I appreciated the warning.

When I was shown to my sales table, I soon discovered I had been paired with an author promoting her new book. She was an atheist. She did not seem to appreciate that she was sharing her space with someone who was a man (strike one) and the producer of a Christian project (strike two).

Later the author's partner, who had listened to our tape of *I Can't Talk about It* and was helping at the sales table, admitted that she liked the songs. She asked me if I had been abused.

I answered truthfully that I had not. "Then how do you know what you know?" she challenged me.

"I prayed and this is what God sent," I replied.

In retrospect it seems such a naïve and simplistic answer, but it was entirely true. I was *not* a survivor. I was *not* a trained, professional counselor. And yet, the songs on the project seemed to continually minister in ways that I could not explain, beyond any expertise other than my ability to craft a song. Much to my surprise, the author, who had been dismissive and condescending to me when we first met, endorsed "Innocent Child" before the weekend was over.

When the time came for the closing ceremonies, all of the conference attendees gathered in a room where three hundred chairs were in a large circle with their backs to the wall. In the middle of the circle was a grand piano. After two women performed a lovely dance, it was time for me to share "Innocent Child."

Apprehensively, I began to sing:

Precious one
I know you've been sad for so long
Don't blame yourself
You didn't do anything wrong
You only wanted attention
Every child needs the same
You are as pure as a flower
In the cleansing rain

It's not your fault
You are an innocent child
It's not your fault
You are an innocent child

I have never passed out, but I think I know what it feels like right before one does. From the very first few lines in the song, I could feel the pain in the room. I could hear women crying all round me, and it felt as if someone were standing behind my back pushing down on my shoulders with both hands. Soon I was having trouble breathing, and I had to slow the song way down and gasp for breath between each line. I wasn't even sure I was going to make it through the song, but managed somehow to carry on.

> *Precious one*
> *I know the nightmares you've had*
> *Don't be ashamed*
> *You didn't do anything bad*
> *You only wanted approval*
> *Every child needs love*
> *You are a perfect creation*
> *of the Holy One*
>
> *It's not your fault*
> *You are an innocent child*
> *It's not your fault*
> *You are an innocent child*[3]

When I was finished, I walked to my chair and buried my head in my hands and sobbed. Not just tears but great wrenching sobs. I had never cried like that before in public. It took me several minutes to compose myself. But when I finally did, I looked up and was presented with a miraculous gift.

A long line of women—the women I'd been told hated to be hugged by men—were lined up *to hug me*.

They all spoke words of appreciation and kindness for the song I shared, but it was the special words of one woman that went deep into my heart.

She said, "People have been telling me I was an innocent child my whole life, but I never believed it until I heard you sing it today."

I knew in that moment that what she said was important. I also knew that there was something else I was supposed to do about it, but I didn't yet know what it was. Looking back later I realized that God used her words to plant the seed that would eventually grow into the ministry of Music for the Soul.

From that point forward the path was clearer. God had given me a call through the words of a woman who had heard the truth in a way she could finally believe, *because of a song*.

The experience at that conference helped me to craft a mission statement for my work, which is this: "My music will reflect the compassionate, healing nature of Christ."

Since then, God has honored that statement in more miraculous ways than I can recount. God has also shown me that music and song, while valued to some degree in our culture, can play a far more important role in healing hurting hearts and setting people free.

Whether musically talented or not, we all have "a song to sing," a voice in sharing God's renewing love with our hurting world. This is because God has graciously given each one of us unique gifts and talents. I believe God wants us to share those gifts with the world. In the process we will not only bless others but ourselves, as well, by living out God's purpose for our lives.

The song "Innocent Child" can be streamed at www.musicforthesoul.org/resources/broken-to-bless.

A Path of God's Design

*"Music is so important. It changes thinking,
it influences everybody, whether they know it or not.
Music knows no boundary lines."*
IRVING BERLIN

The clarity and sense of purpose that my new mission statement brought to my life was amazing. It made assessing opportunities much easier. Either they were in line with my mission statement or they weren't. What was truly surprising to me though was how opportunities in line with my mission statement seemed to find me. It was as if God was saying, "Well since you asked, . . ."

By this time my working relationship with Lynne McCleery at Score Productions had blossomed into a friendship. And so it was that just a short time after I came up with my mission statement, Lynne called me about something that had nothing to do with our TV music work.

One of her dear friends had contracted the HIV virus, developed AIDS, and was now fighting for his life. Lynne was involved with an organization called AIDS LA that was putting together a fund-raiser and asked me if I would write a song for the event.

This was at a time when many prominent voices in the Christian community were calling AIDS God's judgment against homosexuals. I felt from the beginning that, as one who was seeking to follow Christ, my job was to respond with compassion to those stricken with this insidious disease. I told Lynne yes, and over the next few days I wrote a song called "We're All in This Together."

Lynne had said they wanted an up-tempo, Bruce Springsteen-like song for the live event they were planning. Accordingly, the work tape I created was a straight-ahead rock and roll song. When we went into the studio to record the song, however, the singer we had hired sat down at the piano and started playing through the song slowly. He began to sing the vocal in a very bluesy rendition. Instantly the song took on a whole different feeling, and we all realized it worked beautifully as a ballad.

One thing led to another, and soon Lynne and I found ourselves in a different recording studio with the incredibly talented soulful pop and jazz vocalist Patti Austin capturing a ballad version of the song.

As all of this was going on, my wife Meredith and I were praying and talking about whether it was time for us and our toddler-aged daughter to leave Los Angeles. My wife had been working on the ABC television show *Step by Step* and become increasingly troubled by the disrespectful, sarcastic tone with which the teenage characters on the show spoke to their parents. One evening she wondered aloud, "How can I work on a show I wouldn't even let my own children watch?"

We were going back and forth about this while I was working with Stephen Breithaupt on *I Can't Talk about It*. Meanwhile some interesting things were happening with "We're All in This Together."

The NAMES Project AIDS memorial quilt was scheduled to be on display in Washington, DC, that year. The quilt is made up of three-foot-by-six-foot panels created by the loved ones of someone who has died of causes related to AIDS.[1] During the day while the quilt was on display, there was a ceremony where the names of all those represented on the quilt were read aloud. That evening, with the lighted Washington Monument as a backdrop, Patti Austin sang "We're All in This Together" for a crowd of thousands.

It's a family of man we've got on this planet
There isn't one life we can take for granted
Everybody has a mark to leave
A difference to make
Our backs may be against the wall
But our spirit will not break
Is it someone you know or only a stranger?
If we stop to ask then we're all in danger
It takes guts to rise each morning
and look this thing in the eye
The solution starts with love
and a dream that will not die

We're all in this together
There isn't any doubt
We're all in this together
There's no one we can do without
And we'll never give in
'til we knock this thing out
Every star will shine forever
We're all in this together

Don't you ever lose hope
It's our silver lining
As long as we don't give up
We'll make the horizon
Here's to everyone who's brave enough
to keep fighting for life

*Here' to everyone that's working hard
to shed a little light*

Repeat CHORUS²

That was in the summer of '92. Austin went on to record a version of the song for a CD she recorded live at the Bottom Line in New York City. And I thought that was the end of the story.

Not Just Some Crazy Idea

Meanwhile, my wife and I had made the difficult decision. We would leave our family and friends in Los Angeles and move to Nashville, Tennessee. We didn't have jobs in Nashville and knew less than five people who lived there, but we felt that this was a leap of faith we were being led to make.

One of our friends at our Los Angeles church was deeply perplexed by this decision. Week after week he stopped us after the service and said, "So let me get this straight. You have family and friends and jobs *here*. You don't have any family or jobs *there*."

We told him, "We're stepping out in faith, Michael. If it doesn't work out, we can always come back."

Nevertheless, when one jumps off a cliff, one looks for affirmation. I found myself praying, "God, in Your mercy, would You please show me that this is Your leading and not just some crazy idea of mine."

As an avid baseball fan, I'd attended literally hundreds of Dodger games over the years and had never even come close to catching a foul ball. I decided to go to one last game before leaving Los Angeles, and you guessed it. I got my foul ball souvenir. Was this good-bye gift a God wink, or was I reaching for an affirmation?

After a three-day, cross-country trip with my dad driving my pickup truck and my friend Adam Greenman and I taking turns driving the twenty-seven-foot U-Haul jammed with all of our stuff, we pulled into Nashville on a sunny Monday afternoon in late May. I looked in the newspaper and saw that the local Double A baseball team the Nashville Xpress had a home game that evening. "Let's leave the stuff to unload until tomorrow and go enjoy the game tonight," I suggested. So we did.

Even though the vendors at ballparks always cry out, "You *gotta* have a program!" I have never been in the habit of buying one. But since it was my first day in my new city, I decided to get one on this night.

> When one jumps off a cliff, one looks for affirmation.

No sooner had dad, Adam, and I settled into our seats behind the first-base dugout and looked up to see the iconic guitar-shaped scoreboard in center field, than the announcer came over the public address system to give the "winning number for tonight's drawing. Look in your program to see if you're a winner!"

You guessed it. *I* was the winner. I'd received a good-bye gift in my old city *and* a welcome gift in my new city! Was God winking *again*?!

If I had been so inclined, I might have written both of those off as extraordinary coincidences. But then I walked into Tower Records. (This was back in the not-so-long ago day when they still had entire stores committed to selling nothing but music!)

Tower Records on the Sunset strip in Los Angeles had been one of my favorite destinations for many years. You could find *anything* there! I had been in town only a few days before I decided to see how the Nashville Tower Records measured up.

When I walked into the store, I stopped dead in my tracks. Hanging from the ceiling stretching from one side of the store to the other above the CD racks was a banner declaring "We're All in This Together" month at Tower Records. I had been aware that GRP Records was planning to release a multi-artist CD that featured the song, but the Tower promotion was a complete and total surprise. Talk about rolling out the welcome mat!

By this time the concept of coincidence was off the table and providence was in clear view.

Before I left Los Angeles, my friend Lynn Barrington, who had experience working in the Christian music industry, told me about a friend of hers named Steve Reno, who was employed with a Nashville Christian music record company called Starsong. After being in town about ten days, I decided it was time to give Reno a call.

These weren't just "winks." Mountains were moving!

He greeted me warmly but thoughtfully warned me off of any high hopes I might have. He said, "I can't help you on the music side. I work in accounting."

I told him that was OK, that I was going to need friends anyway, and asked if he would still be willing to meet with me. He agreed, and the following day I went to his office at Starsong.

After I arrived we chatted for a while about our mutual friend Lynn, our families, and this and that. Then he asked if I had any songs with me I could play for him. I said, "Sure," and pulled out a copy of "We're All in This Together."

When the song finished playing, he asked me, "Did you write that by yourself?"

"Yes," I replied.

"Wait here," he said and left the room.

When Steve returned, he had Jonathan Watkins, the head of the Starsong music publishing department, with him. I followed Jonathan downstairs to his office where we chatted for a little while. Then he asked to hear "We're All in This Together." When it was over, he repeated the same question Steve had asked me: "Did you write that by yourself?"

I told him yes, and the next thing he asked floored me. "What would it take to get you to sign here?"

I had been in Nashville less than two weeks, and I was being offered a staff songwriting contract! I had expected it would take me at least a year to get connected in the songwriting community, let alone signed to a publishing deal. Within three months, my first songs were recorded by contemporary Christian music artists, and before the year was out I had my first number-one single on CCM radio.*

So often with hindsight we can clearly see how God was moving in a certain area of our lives even though we couldn't see it at the time. Our first few months in Nashville were one of those rare times where I felt God was moving quickly to change our lives, and allowing me to see it in real time! These weren't just "winks." Mountains were moving!

Only God Knows

A few years earlier, while I was working as a DJ in the lounge of the Sheraton Hotel in Industry Hills, California, a lady came up on a particularly slow night and requested a song by Toto. (Remember, I attended high school with several members of that band.) When I pulled out the greatest hits CD to play this lady's request, I was hit with the reality that I had not accomplished my goal of becoming a full-time professional songwriter or musician like my friends had done. "I didn't get to do it," I said out loud to myself. And though there was a melancholy to the realization, I remember thinking, as I played the song to a virtually empty room, *That's OK. I have a good life.*

There is no way I could have known that another evening, just a few years later, I would be sitting in my car in the driveway of my

---

* Contemporary Christian Music; the song was "Hungry for You" by East to West.

Nashville home listening to my song "Father Foundation" on a pre-release copy of the new Willie Davis CD Starsong was putting out. As if picking up a conversation from only a few moments earlier, I suddenly found myself saying out loud to an empty car, "Wait a minute! I *did* get to do it!!" That sobering night a few years earlier at the Sheraton in Industry Hills was *not* the end of the story!

It wasn't until years later that I reflected on the fact that God used a song written for a friend—a song that honored my mission statement—to help me land a staff songwriting deal. My dream had come true after all! But in God's timing and in a way I could never have scripted or imagined. This had been a path of God's design.

God has a design in mind for the life of a song as well. Once a songwriter has written a song and it's out there, it is amazing the way it takes on a life of its own, touching the lives of others in times and places of which the writer is not usually even aware.

Through the years I can tell you that many of the Christian songwriters I've been privileged to work with pray for God's leading in the writing process and commit the work they create into God's hands to be used as God sees fit. In so doing we trust that God can take the songs we've written and use them to bless others and meet the needs in their hearts that only God knows.

As such, we are always grateful when God chooses to give us a glimpse of how a song has impacted someone's life on this side of heaven. It seems that those encouragements usually come on the days when the grind of the business side or some major disappointment—like having a recording artist drop a song that has been on hold*—threatens to wear us down.

Naturally, I had a front-row seat for how "We're All in This Together" changed my own life! But imagine my gratitude when I

---

* *On hold* is a music industry term used to describe a song that an artist is planning to record. A song on hold is not supposed to be played for any other recording artist to consider.

received an e-mail from a college professor in 2012, sharing that he had used "We're All in This Together" to generate dialogue among his students about the Christian response to the AIDS epidemic.

He cited the approach of the song as a contrast to the generally negative tone of many Christian leaders in the early nineties, which got so much attention in the media. I was struck by the fact that many of his students were not even *alive* when the song was written! I was humbled by the opportunity for the message of compassion in the song to reach across time and speak into their lives.

> God has a design in mind for the life of a song.

Then, as recently as 2013, I received another e-mail, this time from Tim, a hospice worker, asking if he could have permission to sing "We're All in This Together" in his church. "It truly is an honor to sing this great song. It has touched me for years and helped me through literally thousands of deaths. I'm glad to be a part of helping this song continue to touch the lives of many others."

When I re-read this e-mail, I can't help but think of how God began honoring my mission statement from the very moment it came to me, helping me to focus my writing and bringing forth opportunities that were in line with the purposes God had in mind for my music.

Theologian Frederick Buechner has been quoted as saying, "The place God calls you to be is the place where your deep gladness and the world's deep hunger meet." Here was a place where the desires of my heart and the talents God had given and nurtured in me could intersect with the needs of people.

And it was only the beginning.

NOT TOO FAR FROM HERE

"The aim and final end of all music should be none other than the glory of God and the refreshment of the soul."
JOHANN SEBASTIAN BACH

A short time after I moved to Nashville, I was scheduling two songwriting appointments per day, one at 10 a.m. and one at 2 p.m. Keeping this schedule I wrote 115 songs my first year in town. I certainly wasn't treating songwriting like a hobby anymore. This was my first opportunity as a staff songwriter, and I was determined to make the most of it.

Starsong, the company that had signed me, was in a two-story building that housed a record company upstairs and a publishing company downstairs. There were three other staff writers: Dwight Liles, writer of "We Are an Offering" and author of more than twenty number-one CCM singles; Randy Holland, writer of Anita Baker's pop smash "Giving You the Best that I've Got"; and Ty Lacy.

Even before I officially signed my deal with Starsong, Ty, who had an uncanny gift for melody and was a prolific idea guy, had been a frequent visitor to my home as he and I began to co-write several times a week. He knew how to give a song that certain something that touches the soul. "It's got to have that ache," he would say to me.

Ty was always on the move, the kind of a guy who was leaving a room almost the moment he entered it. But he had an infectious energy that drew people to him and a virtually bottomless fount of song ideas. If he was coming to a writing meeting, you didn't have to worry about bringing an idea because he would bring several—and most of them would be good.

Usually Ty had part of the melody and a few lines of lyric already worked out, and it wasn't long before he trusted me to finish his ideas. Dozens and dozens of our songs were recorded during my Starsong days.

One day after Ty left my house, I found a yellow notepad he had left behind on my kitchen counter. On it were five words: Not Too Far From Here. There was nothing else on the page. The moment I saw those words I called Ty and said, "I've got dibs on this title. You are writing this song with me!" That might have been the most important phone call I ever made. Because of all of the songs I've been a part of writing, none has been more special than "Not Too Far from Here."

I remember Ty coming over to the house the following morning and sitting down at the piano. He already had the first verse mostly worked out, both melody and lyric. Before long he headed out to another appointment, and I found myself stretched out on the floor working on the second verse. I often find the best lyrics are close to the ground.

As I was writing, the thought came to me that this song was a prayer. Accordingly, after the first and second verses, where the storytelling is observant, the bridge and the last verse shift to become a direct plea to God.

Help me, Lord, not to turn away from pain
Help me not to rest while those around me weep
Give me Your strength and compassion
When somebody finds the road of life too steep[1]

When the song was finished, our publisher felt that a simple piano/vocal demo would be enough to interest a recording artist in the song. Aaron Benward, the soulful young vocalist of the new Starsong duo Aaron Jeoffrey, sang the demo for us, and the song was almost immediately put on hold and subsequently recorded by Kim Boyce for her CD *By Faith*.

A music video was created for the song, and it was singled and went to number one on the Christian inspirational chart early in 1994. So, as appreciative as I was of the song's chart success, I figured that was it for "Not Too Far from Here." I didn't give it much thought as I continued to focus my attention on creating an ever-growing catalog of new songs. But this particular song had only just begun its journey.

Jesus Is Waiting

On April 19, 1995, the Alfred P. Murrah Federal Building in Oklahoma City was bombed, up to that time the most devastating and deadly act of terrorism on American soil. When we heard the news, Ty and I were writing a song with Janice Chaffee in the Word offices at 3319 West End Avenue in Nashville. We immediately stopped to pray, but words were hard to come by.

As the week went on I found myself struck silent every time I tried to pray for the families of the loved ones lost in the bombing, especially the children who were in the day care center. I felt I had no words.

Eight days later on Thursday, April 27, the annual Gospel Music

Awards celebration was held in Nashville. Dove Awards were handed out for the songs and artists voted by the industry as the "best" in Christian music from the previous year.

By this time EMI had bought Starsong so it was that I found myself at the EMI post-awards party in a trendy Nashville eatery on that Thursday night. I was standing and chatting with partygoers when a limousine pulled up carrying some of the award-winning Christian recording artists. Before I had time to react, I was literally shoved out of the way by some photographers angling for pictures of the artists emerging from the limousine.

I felt I had no words.

That was my first experience with Christian paparazzi. It was a startling encounter and left me wondering, *What am I doing here?* The whole scene felt wrong somehow. So, I decided to go home to be with my family.

My mother-in-law was staying with us at the time and had an early flight the following morning. I was returning from the airport, pulling into our driveway, when my five-year-old daughter burst out of the house shouting, "Daddy, Daddy, come quick! Your song is on television!"

I thought, *Why would my family be watching re-runs at this hour?*, thinking she must be referring to a song I'd written for Score Productions back in Los Angeles.

When I stepped into the den, I found my wife sitting on the sofa crying and pointing at the television. There on the TV, on *Good Morning America*, was an eight-year-old girl singing "Not Too Far from Here." As she sang, images of rescue workers helping people out of the rubble of the Murrah federal building appeared on the screen.

I was speechless. I couldn't believe what I was seeing. Then I heard the last line of the song: "Jesus is waiting, not too far from here."

The Christian music industry had not done this. If so, someone would have told me about it in advance.

So how did it come to pass that Mikaila Enriquez from Edmond, Oklahoma, had just sung "Jesus is waiting " on ABC, on network television, for millions of viewers?

In the coming days, I learned from her mother, Pamela, that Mikaila's vocal teacher recently had purchased the sheet music for "Not Too Far from Here" to teach it to Mikaila for an upcoming vocal recital. Mikaila had never sung a solo in church before, but when the pastor's wife at her church called and asked if there was anything Mikaila could sing for the memorial service, she already knew "Not Too Far from Here" by heart. The *MacNeil-Lehrer NewsHour* captured her performance on camera as she sang the song in a church where the bombing had blown out one hundred stained-glass windows.

Pamela was volunteering in the church kitchen a few days later when producers from *Good Morning America* called looking for "the little girl who sang that song on television." It was then they invited her to New York to sing the song on the last broadcast of the week to a nation still hurting in the wake of the horrific event.

Calls to ABC came in by the thousands that day with people asking where they could get a recording of Mikaila singing the song. Of course the answer was that they couldn't. This was not a music industry happening. This was God caring for His people.

Shortly thereafter, Warner Brothers put out a CD entitled *Music from the Oklahoma City Memorial Service* on which "Not Too Far from Here" was included. Later on my friend Jason Deere, an Oklahoma City native, was having dinner with friends in his hometown and mentioned that he knew the writer of the song. One of his friends said, "Tell your friend he will never know what that song has meant to our city."

Hearing that made me think back to when I felt I had no words to pray in the wake of the bombing—and how I felt when I was

writing the lyric to "Not Too Far from Here," that I was writing a
prayer. I was humbled and grateful that God took the words of that
song and used them as a healing balm in the aftermath of such a
terrible tragedy. It turns out I'd had the words after all.

Somebody's down to their last dime
Somebody's running out of time
Not too far from here
Somebody's got nowhere else to go
Somebody needs a little hope
Not too far from here
and I may not know their names
But I'm praying just the same
That You'll use me, Lord, to wipe away a tear
'Cause somebody's crying
Not too far from here

Somebody's troubled and confused
Somebody's got nothing left to lose
Not too far from here
Somebody's forgotten how to trust
Somebody's dying for love
Not too far from here
It may be a stranger's face
But I'm praying for Your grace
To move in me and take away the fear
'Cause somebody's hurting
Not too far from here

Help me, Lord, not to turn away from pain
Help me not to rest while those around me weep
Give me Your strength and compassion
When somebody finds the road of life too steep

Now I'm letting down my guard
and I'm opening my heart
Help me speak Your love to every needful ear
Jesus is waiting
*Not too far from here*²

A Life of Its Own

It also turned out that Michael Crawford, of *The Phantom of the Opera* fame, had heard Mikaila sing the song. And so when he decided to record a CD of spiritual songs in 1998, he included "Not Too Far from Here."

I didn't learn about this until it had already happened. My friend Ray came up to me one night at Jammin' Java, a music club in Franklin, Tennessee, which regularly featured Christian music, and said, "Hey, congratulations on your Michael Crawford cut." My response was a startled, "What?!" While I was grateful for Crawford recording the song, when I finally heard it I was deeply disappointed. He and his team had decided to leave "Jesus" out of his version.

My frustration grew as he sang the song on ABC's *The View*, in his PBS special, and later on a live CD, each time leaving Jesus out of the song.*

However, between Boyce's version of the song, Mikaila's version—recorded later on her first CD—and Crawford's version, "Not Too Far from Here" took on a life of its own.

I heard from a missionary in the jungles of South America for whom the message of the song had been a comfort and sustaining encouragement as she labored through challenging hardships in virtual anonymity.

---

* In recording "Not Too Far from Here" for the Music for the Soul CDs *After the Storm* and *Broken to Bless*, I used Jesus' name in the lyric THREE times!

I heard from Graham Webb, a hair care products executive in England, about how the song was being used in Great Britain for a campaign to stop child abuse.

Several websites appeared online devoted to sharing the lyric of the song, many of them talking about its role in helping people through difficult circumstances. (That is *still* happening all these years later.)

And I heard from Kim Boyce herself about a call she received from a man who reached out to her and shared that her recording of the song brought the hope of Christ to him at just the point when he considered ending his life. She told me, "I believe my whole career was just so I could get to the point where I could sing that song."[3]

To this day, every time I play the song live, someone comes up and tells me a story about what the song has meant to them. I will forever be grateful to Kim for choosing to record it!

Like with "We're All in This Together," God used "Not Too Far from Here" to make an important difference in my life as well. But first I would have to be nudged further in the direction of ministry through an experience I had with yet another of my own songs.

A Call Grows Louder

While I was a staff writer at McSpadden-Smith Music Publishing, I became friends with and wrote some songs for a talented male vocalist they managed named Clay Crosse. Later, when Clay's record label Reunion was getting ready to put together a greatest hits compilation CD, he needed a few new songs for the project.

Clay came to me with an idea he had for a male trio recording. I can still remember us sitting in his car in the parking lot at Cracker Barrel in Nashville listening to a song from the *Miss Saigon* soundtrack. "I want something that captures this kind of feeling musically but that has a strong 'men linking arms for Christ' message."

Back at the music room in my basement, we began writing what would become "I Will Follow Christ." Once the song was completed, Clay invited Bob Carlisle, fresh off of a recent smash with "Butterfly Kisses," and BeBe Winans to sing the song with him.

> I would never be able to view my Christian songwriting career in the same way again.

"I'm going to make it a car chase," producer Regie Hamm told me, sharing his vision for creating an exciting recording. Not only did he deliver an incredible production, but he also, though not taking credit as a songwriter, made a critically important improvement in the chorus lyric.

It was once again Gospel Music Association week, and I knew that Clay was planning on unveiling the song at a live event. So on Monday night April 19, 2000, I found myself sitting in the world-famous Ryman Auditorium in downtown Nashville for a GMA week kick-off concert featuring several contemporary Christian recording artists.

When Clay took center stage, he was alone and quietly began to sing the opening strains of the song. The tone in the audience was that respectful, yet restrained, feeling that always greets recording artists when they are singing a song the audience doesn't know.

Then, emerging from the wings stage left and singing the first line of the second verse as he entered, came Bob Carlisle. The excitement meter in the crowd jumped several notches. Clay Crosse and Bob Carlisle together! The crowd was into it now, new song or not.

Then as the second chorus came to an end, out from stage right stepped BeBe Winans. And as BeBe began to sing the following lines, the only way to put it is that the crowd in the Ryman simply went bananas.

I behold your life and see the man you want me to become
Someone who belongs to the kingdom that was sealed
 on Calvary
I will tell the world what I believe[4]

As the "car chase" reached its crescendo, with the three singers giving it their all, the entire audience rose to their feet screaming and applauding before the song was even over. I sat in the middle of all of this and thought simply, *Wow.*

The very next morning the Columbine massacre happened.

In the days following the shooting, it was reported that one of the victims had been asked if she believed in God and was shot when she replied, "Yes."

When I heard that, it rocked me to the core. In the coming weeks as I reflected on what had happened, I found myself thinking, *When I say I will follow Christ, I get a standing ovation for my song, a hit single on the radio, and make money. This young lady says it and is killed.*

I would never be able to view my Christian songwriting career in the same way again. Don't get me wrong. I was grateful for the success I was having. Every songwriter wants his or her songs to be heard and appreciated. And it was a dream come true to be making my living doing what I had always wanted to do. But this sequence of events deeply unsettled me.

Oh, I trusted that God would use the song. Clay confirmed as much, telling me in a phone call later that "I Will Follow Christ" received a big response in concert every night and that people had come forward to give their hearts to Christ after hearing the song. Because he had a chance to sing it in his concerts, he had an ongoing positive relationship with the song that I didn't have.

The song continued to represent something disquieting for me—a commercialization of my beliefs with which I was increasingly uncomfortable. I began to consistently feel a conflict between the message in the songs and the model of the industry. This feeling only increased when, on top of everything else, the song won a Dove Award for inspirational song of the year. The ministry call was growing louder. When asked to play the song at writers' nights, I would decline, and it was more than ten years before I felt that I could play the song with any authenticity.

Within the contemporary Christian music industry, I was privileged to work with supremely talented people who were committed Christians. For a decade I met, collaborated, and ultimately developed deep friendships with some of the most incredible people of faith I have ever known. I cherish those friendships to this day. But I could feel that this season was coming to a close. Once again, I felt God was now calling me to do a new thing with music.

So it was that by 2000 I was seriously considering leaving my career as a contemporary Christian music staff songwriter to start a ministry using songs to help people dealing with life's toughest challenges.

But considering—even seriously considering—is not the same thing as *doing*. Sometimes we need God to give us one more swift kick, to make it so obvious that we have no other choice. For me that kick came in the form of a black-tie dinner invitation.

One day a woman approached me at church. Bill Tallent, one of the men in our congregation, was going to be honored at a formal dinner affair at the University Club at Vanderbilt for his role in having started a Nashville-based Christian counseling center some fifteen years earlier. Apparently "Not Too Far from Here" was one of his favorite songs, and this woman from church asked me if I would be willing to come to the event and sing the song for Bill. I replied that I would be honored. Then she told me the room where the dinner would be taking place didn't have a piano. This made me slightly uncomfortable since I had written the song on the piano and had never played it on the guitar. But since I was being asked to do this for Bill, I decided to accept anyway.

The night of the event I arrived with my guitar in hand only to find that the room where I was to sing had no sound system to speak of, only a podium with a microphone attached. Now I was *really* uncomfortable. But the show must go on, right? So, because I was supposed to be there to play the song for Bill, that's what I did, pulling a chair up in front of Bill's table and singing the song directly to him without the help of a microphone.

> I felt God was now calling me to do a new thing with music.

After I sang the song and went back to sit at my table, I found myself asking God, "What am I doing here, Lord?" For the most part, the couples at this event traveled in a different stratum of society than my wife and I did. Even though I'd been invited to sing, I felt completely out of place. Still, I had the sense that the Lord was trying to show me something.

Speaker after speaker came up to the podium to extol Bill for his role in bringing about the Vine Street Christian Counseling Center and to praise him for the thousands of hours of help given to members of the Nashville community because of his efforts. And then it landed on me like a ton of bricks.

Steve, whose permission are you waiting for?

I thought, *In fifteen years, if someone were to throw a dinner on your behalf, what would they say?* I knew right then and there in that room that I was being shown that it would take a leap of faith—not unlike the one we took when we left Los Angeles—for the music ministry I envisioned to be born.

The House with No Visible Means of Support

On the way home in the car, I said to my wife, "Honey, I think it's time for me to leave my cushy publishing deal and start the ministry." Although my wife was in graduate school at the time and my staff deal was our primary source of income, she said without hesitation, "Go for it."

When we were newlyweds, often passing up secure, better-paying jobs to follow our dreams, we called ourselves "the house with no visible means of support." God always met our needs, usually at the last minute and in miraculous ways. But now we had two children. It seemed much more risky. Her support of my dream was evidence of the strength of her faith.

The Sunday morning following the dinner a woman came forward toward the end of the worship service to join the church. When introducing her to the congregation, the pastor said, "Jenny works to help not-for-profit charities and philanthropists dialogue."

I thought, *Well,* of course *she does.*

God was putting just the person I needed right in front of me at precisely the moment I needed her. This was the first of many times that this would happen.

I approached Jenny after church and told her that I was going to start a ministry and asked her if she would meet with me. The following week we met for coffee, and by the end of our time together, I had two full pages of notes on a legal pad. Following those notes to a tee resulted in Music for the Soul being successfully incorporated exactly one year later.

Now that this decision had been made, I figured it was time to tell Shawn McSpadden, my dear friend and publisher at Word. Over the course of three years, he and I had worked, along with another dear friend, John Mandeville, on a series of original children's recordings for Tyndale House called *Kidz Tunz.*[5]

Shawn and I were flying up to Chicago for a meeting about the children's music when I told him that I was going to turn my focus to full-time ministry. "Are you sure you want to do that?" he asked. When I assured him that I was certain and that my mind was made up, he said, "OK, but I think you're crazy." But even though he had his reservations, he pledged his support for my decision.*

As it turned out, our meetings in Chicago went much more quickly than we imagined and wrapped up soon after lunchtime. Although we didn't have a flight until 5 p.m., we decided to call a car to go to the airport in hopes of getting on an earlier flight and making it home in time for dinner with our families.

When we got in the car, the driver said, "There's someone in the Wheaton area who also wants to go to Midway. Do you mind if we swing by and pick him up?"

Since our scheduled flight wasn't for several hours, we told him that would be fine. When the next passenger got into the car, we exchanged pleasantries and I asked him, "What do you do for a living?"

He replied, "I raise funds for not-for-profit Christian charities."

I thought, *Well,* of course *you do.*

Think about it. This man, Douglas Shaw, who ran the only company of its kind in a *ten-state area*, was in the same car only because our meeting had ended early. Our original plan had us leaving for the airport two hours later. Also, I had just told Shawn earlier that morning about my decision to start a ministry. Otherwise I would not have felt comfortable speaking freely with Doug about my plans. Coincidence or God's providence?

In the coming months and years Doug helped educate me about fund-raising, and graciously offered the services of his company[6] to help Music for the Soul take its first steps as a ministry. In the process he became a mentor, a supporter, and most importantly, a personal friend.

Once I made the decision to step out in faith and begin Music for the Soul, the next person I needed in the process was "not too far from here," no matter where "here" was.

---

* McSpadden later served as a Music for the Soul board member.

It reminds of me of what my friend Christian counselor Larry Watkins says:

"Jesus knows *everybody*!"

"Not Too Far from Here" may be streamed at
www.musicforthesoul.org/resources/after-the-storm

and

www.musicforthesoul.org/resources/broken-bless/.

5

CIRCLE OF FRIENDS

"I think music in itself is healing. It's an explosive expression
of humanity. It's something we are all touched by.
No matter what culture we're from, everybody loves music."
BILLY JOEL

Well, Billy's mostly right. My wife Meredith might be the one
exception. If you ask her she will tell you, "Music is annoying."
This is highly ironic as she grew up with music in the home. Her
stepfather was a guitar player and songwriter in the band Spanky
and Our Gang back in the sixties. "Like to Get to Know You,"
"Lazy Day," and "Sunday Will Never Be the Same" were a few
of their hits. She actually remembers being back stage at the Ed
Sullivan Show in New York as a nine-year-old.

When we were first dating, I came over to her apartment one
time and thought I heard music playing. Sure enough an album
was spinning on the turntable, but the music was so faint I couldn't
make out who the artist was. As one who prefers music to be the
focal point whenever it's playing, I was dumbfounded. "Are you
going to tell me you're *listening* to that?!"

The joke in our house became that Meredith liked to listen to
music so that you could hear the needle scratching on the record
above the actual song. Of course that was back in the day when we

still listened to records that were pressed on vinyl. There were a few notable exceptions through the years. Dan Fogelberg and Elton John both always had the privilege of being played at an audible level!

Because she grew up around a rock band, the fact that I had success as a songwriter was never a big deal to my wife. For her it was just "the family business." My favorite story happened at our church in Nashville. I was in the midst of a good string of hits and had been asked to play at church a few times. One morning after I shared a song, a woman came up to Meredith and gushed, "It must be so wonderful to be married to such a talented, sensitive songwriter."

Nonplussed, my wife replied, "His socks smell like everybody else's."

The fact that my wife is not particularly a music fan—or when it comes to my career, a Steve fan—has actually been quite helpful to me over the years. I know she always will tell the truth when I ask for her opinion. If a song passes the Meredith test, then it is probably going to meet with approval from the broader audience.

A Pebble in the Pond

We've all heard the phrase "Everything you put out comes back to you." Perhaps in pop music the most notable characterization of this idea came from the Beatles in the last line from *Abbey Road*: "The love you take is equal to the love you make."

In God's amazing creation of the physical world, there is a quick experiment anyone can do that illustrates this. Take a pebble and throw it into a pond. If you stand there long enough, you will notice the ripples eventually come all the way back and touch the shore.

But think about it. The ripples don't reach back and touch the shore only right in front of you. They form concentric circles that eventually touch the shore around the *entire* circumference of the pond!

What if the "love we make" is like that. What if it expands exponentially?

In December 2013 after one customer paid for the coffee of the next person in line at the drive-through window of a Connecticut Starbucks, more than one thousand customers followed suit![1]

That sounds like the kingdom of God to me.

True, we may not always see it. But what if *every* act of kindness we extend replicates itself over and over again and eventually reaches out not just in one direction but in all directions? That sounds like the kingdom of God to me.

I didn't realize it at the time, but that was what was happening when I was working in the contemporary Christian music industry. I was tossing out pebbles every day. Some pebbles were in the form of songs. Others were in the form of conversations shared and relationships formed. Still others were in the form of prayers.

Some of the ripples came back to the shore quickly. For example, only a few months after my song "One Million Reasons" had been released, a woman told me how the song came on the radio in the hospital as she was sitting at her mother's bedside.[2] It was a great comfort to her and helped her to trust God during a very difficult time.

Other ripples took longer to touch the shore. Write About Jesus[3] is a wonderful Christian songwriting workshop put on by multi-award-winning songwriter Sue C. Smith. It takes place every October in St. Charles, Missouri, a suburb of St. Louis. After I'd been leading classes there for several years, a young woman came up to me and told me how Music for the Soul was inspiring her. "You've shown us that you can write songs about things that matter."

The irony is that by far the most successful song in my catalog in terms of notoriety is "Circle of Friends," recorded by Point of Grace. I didn't realize what a metaphor it would become in my own life.

While writing for Christian recording artists, I often felt that the work was sort of parallel to the mission statement God had given me for my life but not really spot-on. After all, while some of my songs spoke of the healing and compassion of Christ, many did not. It seemed as if I spent a lot of time creating the message that *other* people—recording artists, record labels, and radio stations—wanted to share.

While I understand the intent and value behind a radio station having the motto "safe for the whole family,"* I longed to create songs that dealt more honestly and consistently with the things that cause deep pain in people's lives. I appreciated the hit songs and the awards—after all, everybody likes for his work to be recognized and praised—but I couldn't escape the feeling that in many ways I had simply traded one genre of the music business for another.

In *Teaching a Stone to Talk*,[4] Annie Dillard writes about how instead of dressing up in our Sunday best for church we should be wearing crash helmets and life jackets. Dillard's observation confirmed something I'd experienced. For example, one morning a woman came up to me at our church and asked, "How are you doing?" When I began to answer honestly that I was struggling because of an illness in the family, she started to physically *back away from me!* She wanted the typical surface-level-Sunday-morning pleasantries. I needed a life jacket!

Discontented with settling for safeness in my work, I was longing to put on the crash helmet! I wanted my music to intentionally minister to people going through life's most difficult and messy situations.

---

* Salem Radio Network's branding slogan for several of its stations

When I finally decided to take the leap of faith to start the ministry of Music for the Soul, I began to see something. My circle of friends included world-class singers, musicians, arrangers, engineers, radio personnel, and music publishers. The pebbles I had tossed into the pond over the previous decade now came back to me in a flood of support, good will, and eagerness to participate and help with the ministry.

During my ten years as a Christian music industry staff songwriter, God had been preparing the team that He would use to bring the ministry to life.

A Questionable Motive

There is another, and somewhat unflattering, irony to this story as well. The fact is, when I wrote "Circle of Friends," my intent was, though not mercenary exactly, certainly financially motivated.

I was in a period where I'd been doing a lot of lyric writing and was ready to take a break and just do some music writing. So I called my friend Scott Krippayne and asked him if he knew any writers who focused primarily on lyrics. He suggested I get in touch with Douglas McKelvey.

Douglas and I met at a coffee shop in a Nashville bookstore, and after some preliminary get-to-know-you conversation, he laid out twenty or thirty lyric sheets on the table for me to comb through. Immediately after I read the lyric to "Circle of Friends," I thought of Point of Grace, who at the time was one of the biggest-selling acts in Christian music.

In my mind's eye, I could see the four young women in the group holding hands and forming a circle. Then I imagined a group of women gathered at a church retreat joining hands to make a prayer circle. I felt instantly that it needed to have the feel of something simple, like a song you would sing around a campfire. The melody to the chorus was in my head by the time I got to my car.

As soon as I got home, I hurried to my office and pulled out my guitar. In ten minutes the song was done.

Soon after, I was blessed to learn that Point of Grace was actually going to record the song. It appeared as the closing track on the platinum-selling album *Life, Love, & Other Mysteries* and was a number-one single, one of twenty-five in a row for the group.

"Even when you forget your mission statement, I remember."

By God's grace the circle of friends made by the song itself reached far and wide. I saw a video of the girls performing the song at a White House prayer breakfast with the unlikely combination of President George W. Bush and Bono in attendance. Still later, country legend Kenny Rogers recorded the song with Point of Grace joining him on the recording. And on YouTube a group of young women performed a version of it in Chinese!

A few years after its release, I saw "Circle of Friends" on an online list of the ten most popular graduation songs. I even heard from a friend of mine who attended a church retreat where the women held hands to form a large circle and sing the song, exactly as I had imagined!

But it was something more up close and personal that affected me the most deeply.

In 2001 Point of Grace was touring in support of *Free to Fly*, their newest CD at the time. I'd never seen them in concert before, and they were scheduled to perform at a large church in Madison, Tennessee, just north of Nashville. One day I was speaking with Shelley Breen, a member of the group, and she said, "You ought to come. We do a request portion during the show every night, and someone always asks for 'Circle of Friends.'"

The night of the performance my family and I drove up to Madison and found seats about two-thirds of the way back from the stage. Toward the end of the concert, the house lights came up, and Shelley began asking the audience what songs they would like to hear.

All of sudden, from behind me, a large group of young women all seated together shouted in unison, "CIRCLE OF FRIENDS!" I later learned they were from Mercy Ministries, a Christian inpatient-counseling clinic in Nashville. I was told that "Circle of Friends" had become an important unifying song for these young ladies, helping to create a bond for them in their recovery.

> *If you weep, I will weep with you*
> *If you sing for joy the rest of us*
> *Will lift our voices too*
> *But no matter what you feel inside*
> *There's no need to pretend*
> *That's the way it is in this circle of friends*[5]

I was immediately humbled that I'd been a part of writing something that was blessing these girls in their healing journey. But I was also a bit ashamed. Remember, I'd written this song primarily in hopes of making money. And I had. It was the best-selling song in my entire catalog. But that night I felt like God was saying, "Steve, even when you forget your mission statement, *I* remember."

God had taken my less-than-pure intentions and done something beautiful for these girls, using the song to share the compassion and healing of Christ.

It was only a few months later that Music for the Soul was incorporated. Since then, I always commit every songwriting and recording session to the Lord, praying that whatever is created is something that God can use to bless whomever He has in mind. I know that I can trust His motives far more than my own.

How Much You Can Give

With the paperwork done and the ministry incorporation coming to fruition, it was time to get serious about how I was going to replace the income I would no longer be receiving from Word. It was also time to get serious about how I was going to let people know about the ministry.

The great thing about a circle of friends is that every time you make a new friend your influence expands as you become part of their network and vice versa.

I was visiting with Regie Hamm one day, and he asked me if I was aware of a group called the Goads. "They're a singing group, but they also have a great ministry," he said. He suggested I contact Rick Goad, one of the brothers in the group, and share with him about my plans for a music ministry.

Rick was based out of Orlando, Florida, but he was coming to the Nashville area in the next few weeks, and so we made plans for he and I and another mutual friend, songwriter and music producer Jim Cooper, to meet at J. Alexander's in Franklin for dinner.

I laid out for Rick in thorough detail my vision for a ministry that would use songs to "talk" to people about things that are often difficult to talk about in church.

"We all build walls to protect ourselves from pain. Music has a way of seeping through the cracks in those walls and softening a heart that has closed itself off. Once that heart opens, you can take a lyric with a healing message and lay it in that open heart," I explained.

Because Rick was a musician and a songwriter, he understood the power of music and seemed interested, so I pressed on.

"Melody is a memory device. By putting the healing message of the lyric with a melody, you have a much better chance that people will remember the message. In fact, one study showed that people remember 10 percent of what they're told, 40 percent of what they read, and 90 percent of what they hear in music."[6]

Once I finished my pitch, Rick leaned in. "You know what I love about this?" he asked.

I couldn't wait to hear.

"When Jesus fed the 5,000, He didn't ask first if they were Democrats or Republicans. He didn't ask if they were Baptists or Presbyterians. He didn't ask if they were black or white. He said the people are hungry. Feed them. You're doing the same thing with music. The people are hurting. Show them compassion!"

Jesus knows everybody.

I gave him some paperwork I'd put together, and we parted with Rick's promise to get together the next time we were in town. My Word deal was only a few weeks from ending when Rick and I met again, this time for breakfast, at his hotel during one of his next visits to town.

"What is Word paying you per year?" he asked.

I told him. Rick promptly replied, "I'll pay you that much per year to write songs with us. We'll bring you down to Orlando every couple of months for a few days to write some songs. The rest of the time you can spend working on Music for the Soul."

I couldn't believe it. God had used someone I hadn't even known just a few months earlier to replace my entire annual income.

Jesus knows everybody. I guess that makes our circle of friends even larger than we realize, doesn't it?

I worked with the Goads during the next couple of years, traveling back and forth to Orlando to write songs for their CD projects. During that time I saw an incredibly talented family and an amazing ministry up close. Their music ministry was only a part of what they brought to the world. While I was there I saw Goad International help people around the globe by providing food, clothing, and medicine, as well as more than seven million Bibles!

In 2006 Rick was diagnosed with terminal cancer, and he went home to be with the Lord in January 2007. But to this day he has a hand in every life touched by Music for the Soul and in countless other lives through the music he recorded, the encouragement he gave, and the commitment that he lived out every day through his work in ministry—that "life is not about how much you can get but how much you can give."

God used Rick to supply what was needed at a pivotal point in the life of Music for the Soul. That is true of so many who have generously given their time, talent, and treasure. The Music for the Soul circle of friends is broad and connected in ways that I can't even see or always understand.

A game I like to play reminds me of the interconnectedness of God's people. It's the "Why do I know this person?" game. I simply think of someone who is important to me and has enriched my life beyond measure. Then I think to myself, *Who introduced me to that person?*

Then, *And who introduced me to* that *person?*, and so on down the line. Invariably, when I get ten or twenty people down the line, I realize that the path to the people who have had the most impact on my life has always begun with a relationship that was brief and, at the time, seemingly unimportant. Often a passing acquaintance has ultimately led to the most significant relationships in my life. For example, Lisa Cobb, an acquaintance that I haven't seen or spoken to in twenty-five years, is responsible for every single relationship I have in Christian music.

Lisa and I attended the Little Brown Church in the Valley at the same time back in the late 1980s, and we both attended a small midweek service led by Rev. Larry Keene. About twenty-five people were usually there. One Wednesday evening after I played one of my songs, Lisa came up to me and said, "You should talk to my friend Lynn Barrington."

So I did. Lynn was very good at spotting what could make a song better. She gave me great input on a lot of my songs, and we became good friends. Then later, when my wife and I decided to move Nashville, it was Lynn who mentioned Steve Reno at Starsong. Everything else in Nashville came from that connection!

Each year there is a Gospel Music Week in Nashville. When I was a signed staff writer, we were expected to attend and "work" the room, speaking with artists, managers, and producers to make connections that could lead to getting our songs heard and recorded. Naturally everybody there had their eye out for the people who could help them the most. It was common for people to be shaking your hand and looking over your shoulder at the same time to see if there was somebody "more important" they should be talking to. A friend of mine called it the "is that Amy Grant behind you?" handshake.

One year Dwight Liles suggested we make a pledge to each other. "Let's promise to look in the eye of the person we are talking to this week for the entire conversation." It was hard, but we pulled it off!

Of course each of us should look everyone we speak with in the eye, treating all people like they matter and as if they are worthy of respect simply because they are one of God's children. But if you're inclined to look for a self-serving reason why you should be interested in the person right in front of you, might I suggest it's because God just may have it in mind to use a "nobody" to change your life. This is a rhetorical example of course. In God's kingdom there is no such thing as a nobody!

During a scene in the 1939 movie *The Wizard of Oz*, Dorothy and her friends are cowering before what they perceive to be the wizard, as he condescendingly thunders orders at them. Dorothy's dog Toto runs off to one side and tugs away at a curtain, pulling it back to reveal a man who is frantically operating levers and shouting into a microphone. "Pay no attention to that man behind the curtain," the con man calls out. Dorothy and her friends now see the truth.

The source of ultimate truth, God is the complete opposite of a con man. But I'm grateful for the times when God has "pulled back the curtain" and let me see all the remarkable ways my life has been changed through the love and generous spirit of friends, colleagues, and acquaintances He has placed in my path. What a great gift it is to be reminded of the truth that our circle of friends is much wider than any of us realize.

WHY A SONG?

*"If you want to touch somebody deeply,
sing to them."*
DR. JOHN OPSATA

The elements of a song—rhythm, melody, harmony, and language—are in us and around us every day. Neurologist Daniel Levitin says, "The part of the brain where music goes to directly [is] related to your deep emotions."[1] When you add melody and lyric together, you begin to get a sense of why a song is so uniquely qualified to communicate with human beings on issues that matter most deeply to them.

Rhythm

Rhythm is at the core of the life that God has given to us, beginning with our heartbeat—the rhythm of blood pulsing through our veins, the rhythm of our breathing, the rhythm of our movements, the rhythm of our speaking. In the natural world we hear rhythms in events as diverse as the pitter-patter of falling rain, the hooves of galloping wild horses striking the ground, and the rumbling of thunder in the atmosphere.

Melody

Air being pushed back and forth is what gives rise to the vibrations that we call sound. The variations in vibration that occur when a stringed instrument is plucked or bowed (or in the case of a piano, struck) or that occur when air is blown through a brass instrument or through the reed of a wind instrument are all perceived as different pitches—notes—by our brain. We hear pitches every day in man-made sounds like the thrum of our car engine, in natural sounds like the songs of birds, and even in our own speech. If you don't think there is melodiousness to speech, try speaking a sentence with all the words on one single tone, and you will hear how inhuman it sounds.

Harmony

Merriam-Webster describes *harmony* as "the combination of different musical notes played or sung at the same time to produce a pleasing sound." We experience the simultaneous sounding of pitches in the natural world all the time. The howling of the wind is full of harmonious overtones, as is the sound of a wave rushing toward or retreating from the beach or the water tumbling over rocks in a river.

So it is these three elements above, in and around us every day of our lives, that when combined with language in the form of a lyric give birth to God's great gift of song. Small wonder, then, that we so naturally respond to a song. It is literally composed of elements that we encounter every day, even *before* our birth!

Dr. Sheila C. Woodward,[2] whose research focus is music and well-being, has been able to show that at seventeen to nineteen weeks a fetus can hear the rhythm of blood rushing through the uterine artery. Elements of rhythm and harmony are in this. She also did a study where she put a microphone and a camera in the womb and was able to prove that "music itself is audible in the womb." The fetus is seen smiling in response to the sound of Woodward's voice.[3]

I have personal experience with this. When my wife became pregnant with our first child, I felt a little envious. Sure, *we* were pregnant, but my wife obviously had an advantage over me in terms of connection. I wanted the baby to have a connection with me as well, one that extended beyond the bloodline and into actual relationship. So I decided to try a musical experiment. Night after night I got close to my wife's abdomen, and I sang:

Jesus loves me this I know
For the Bible tells me so
Little ones to Him belong
They are weak but He is strong
Yes, Jesus loves me
Yes, Jesus loves me
Yes, Jesus loves me
The Bible tells me so

I did this for several months.

I was in the room with my wife when our daughter Stephanie was born. Immediately one of the nurses, sounding concerned, said, "Doctor, look at this." One of our daughter's arms was limp at her side. The doctor suspected she might have a dislocated shoulder as a result of having come through the birth canal. The nurse tightly swaddled my daughter and allowed me to come with her when she took Stephanie and placed her in a hospital crib in a nearby room. I stood over my brand-new baby girl who was screaming and turning a lovely combination of red and purple and softly sang:

Jesus loves me
This I know…

Stephanie looked up at me, or at least in the direction of my voice, and stopped crying.

Admitting My Bias

All forms of art are invaluable.

All forms of art are a different way for us to tell and communicate our stories. They are different channels through which we express our humanity. They are different ways of knowing and understanding who we are. The Bible tells us in Genesis that we are made in the image of God. It follows then that, being made in the image of the ultimate Creator, we are creative beings. And just as God has put great variety into creation, there is great variety in the way people create and communicate.

Some of us are visual learners. We learn by seeing, and so perhaps a dance or a painting will speak to our hearts more than a novel. Some of us learn through stories, so perhaps the poet or the playwright will connect with us more deeply than the work of a sculptor. Some of us learn by doing, so perhaps we need to *be* the writer, the dancer, the actor, or the painter.

When these art forms are combined is when we have some of our most powerful experiences—a great film may include wonderful storytelling, terrific acting, beautiful cinematography, a soaring music score, and inspirational songs, even a dance sequence. A ballet tells a story that includes music, dancing, costumes, and set design.

A great novel, a great film, a great ballet, and a great song all have one thing in common. They tell a story. In this aspect, they reflect Jesus, who was the consummate Storyteller. But, if I may—and admitting my bias as a songwriter—let me extol the virtues of the song for just a moment.

First of all, a song is born through a songwriter who is a story-teller. The best songwriters write their story and yours, even if the song itself is about some third person. There is a universality of language and understanding in a great lyric that is an art form all in itself. It is an art form that draws you inside its own world and makes you realize it's your world, too, as you remember places you've been, emotions you've felt, and things you've seen.

Yes, things you've seen. A songwriter is also an artist, an artist with words. My friend Joel Lindsey teaches a wonderful class called "Song Painting" every year at Write About Jesus. A great song helps us *see* the story by using word pictures to create mental imagery that simultaneously engages our minds and our emotions.

> "A song makes you feel a thought."

A songwriter also paints with music. It is through the music that he or she is able to change the "color" of the words, adding layers of richness and meaning that expand the emotional range and tone of the lyric.

Award-winning lyric writer E. Y. Harburg, probably best known for writing the words to "Somewhere Over the Rainbow," captured the essence of what makes a song so special when he said, "Words make you think a thought. Music makes you feel a feeling. A song makes you feel a thought."

Once the song is ready to be recorded, a whole host of other art forms come in to play. To use a film analogy, a music producer is like a cinematographer, a set designer, and a costume designer all rolled into one. Through the choice of musical arrangements, musicians, singers, equipment, the recording studio and recording engineers, the producer puts together a specific version of the song that the listener will experience.

The lead vocalist, in effect, is an actor. If she does her job well, she will deliver a compelling presentation of the song, adding layers of understanding and emotion to the words she sings through her interpretation of the lyric.

The final result from the participation of all of these people is something that transports us into a new mental and emotional space and "speaks" for us in a language beyond words alone.

Something Changes

It is no accident that songs are such a large part of all worship services, regardless of the style preference. When a song is sung, something changes. If you are the one singing, you can feel it immediately in your body and spirit. If you are the one listening, it might be more gradual, but the change is there nonetheless. Something wakes up inside of us when the singing starts.

A song can bring almost instantaneous joy. It can surprise us with tears. If it's not our type of music, it can even agitate us—perhaps displeasing but still a change!

If we are tense, the right song can relax us. If we're sad, the right song can cheer us up. If we're angry, the right song can defuse our anger. If we're bored, the right song can stimulate us. And so on.

A song can be used to capture a mood. Or chase one away. But regardless of the goal, a song engages us. It interacts with us and we with it. It gets to our core.

One afternoon when I was first talking to clergy members about beginning the ministry of Music for the Soul, I was speaking with Disciples of Christ pastor Dan Moseley.[4] We were discussing the power of a song to break down the barriers that people put up to protect themselves from pain. He said, "You must be careful to melt walls and not blow them up."

Accordingly, from that day forward I have always handled every song and every topic with an extra special degree of care.

Songs can be a balm. Songs can inspire. Songs can be used to educate or, as in the case of protest songs from the folk and rock genres, to activate change. And of course, some songs are just for fun. But they should never be used as dynamite, cavalierly speaking about difficult issues in a way that is hurtful, triggering, or makes light of pain.

What's a Song Worth?

In 2007 *Newsweek* magazine published an article with the headline "How Much Is Music Worth?" It talked about the advent of technology and quoted Princeton professor Ed Felton as saying, "Sometime in the next decade, we'll see a $100 device that fits in your pocket and holds all the music ever recorded by humanity. Copyright owners would be hard-pressed to fight such a system."

The article's author Steven Levy went on to suggest that advances in technology were making it irrelevant to argue what music is worth. "Technology wants to make it close to free."

There is no question that advances in technology and the music industry's slowness to recognize which way the wind was blowing have resulted in decimating the profitability of the music industry as it was once configured. Physical record stores have gone the way of the dinosaur. The album itself is fighting for survival as an art form. The average consumer now expects to pay a whopping $1.29 or less for a song. For many, that only applies if they can't find a way to get it for nothing.

In a September 2014 blog post songwriter Regie Hamm argues, "Content is officially not the thing. The THING (the device) is the thing. Content is just something in the air. It's simply too easy to obtain . . . that's why it no longer has value." Speaking strictly in terms of financial value, it would seem he is right.

But while the marketplace may have decided that a song is worth far less than a cup of coffee, there is another question worth asking. Is what the market will bear the only factor in determining something's real value?

We don't pay for the air we breathe. We don't pay for sunlight. We don't pay for rain. Are any of these things, all gifts from a loving God, worthless because they aren't monetized?

Conversely, in a culture that disproportionately rewards actors and sports stars and often grossly overpays its CEOs, are big dollars a sign of real value or only an indication of what a particular market will pay at a particular time?

"Music . . . reaches where most of us cannot go."

I suggest that, especially where a person's mental and spiritual well being are concerned, it is important, even critical, to look beyond market value and look to the transformative, life-giving value of all forms of art and human expression. And at the top of this list would be music.

Dr. Oliver Sacks was a New York-based neurologist who did extensive studies on the power of music. In an article called "When Music Heals,"[5] he wrote, "Responsiveness to music is an essential part of our neural nature." That essentialness suggests worth.

The value expands when one speaks of a song. Daniel Levitin says in *This Is Your Brain on Music*, "As a tool for activation of specific thought music is not as good as language. As a tool for arousing feelings and emotion music is better than language. And the combination of the two as best exemplified in a song is best of all."[6]

I think another important point to be considered is context. The discussion of all the different ways that songs bless our lives found in chapter 2 illustrates that how, when, and where a song is shared directly impacts the value that a song adds in any given situation. To say that elevator music is worthless, for example, is a point that might be successfully argued. To say that a song providing therapeutic breakthrough on an issue with which one has struggled for a lifetime is worthless is, of course, absurd. If music, as one therapist friend of mine put it, "permeates our souls," then its value in such settings is incalculable.

When speaking to me about the effectiveness of the Music for the Soul ministry, Tennessee therapist Dr. David Walley said, "Music . . . reaches where most of us cannot go."

Wendy Farley, a professor at Emory University in Atlanta, Georgia, says, "If I were the best writer in the world I couldn't do what music can do."

Philosopher Suzanne K. Lager says, "The real power of music lies in the fact that it can be 'true' to the life of feeling in a way that language cannot."[7]

And Levitin again, "The multitude of reinforcing cues of a good song; rhythm, melody, and contour cause music to stick in our heads and that's the reason why . . . the Old Testament [was] set to music in preparation for being passed down by oral tradition across the generations."[8]

Reverend John Feldhacker, pastor of Edgehill United Methodist Church in Nashville, was responding to our music when he called Music for the Soul "ministry in the truest sense of the word. I have not seen anything more meaningful and effective in modeling the nature of the love God has for real people experiencing very real struggles and brokenness in today's world."

The essence of the comments from these five individuals—a therapist, a professor, a philosopher, a neurologist, and a pastor—all support the same conclusion. Namely, that music—regardless of what the current economic price tag may be—is, in fact, priceless.

Beware Delegitimizing

Because you are reading this book, I have reason to believe that you agree that there is something to this music/song thing or are at the very least interested in the idea that there might be. You've experienced and appreciated its power in your own life. You've seen that a song can impact a life, a congregation, and a community. Well, what if you wanted to *dis*-empower this form of communication? What if you wanted to invalidate music and songs and render them ineffective? And if that were your goal, how successful would you be at accomplishing that goal if you were able to convince the world that music was worthless? That a song had no value?

Some might accuse me of over-spiritualizing the issue at this point, in effect trying to make something a religious issue that really isn't. But I offer for your consideration that there is an enemy of our spirits who would like nothing better than for us to consider music worthless.

In John 10:10 it says this enemy seeks to kill and destroy, and anything that unites us corporately in an activity that lifts our spirits and brings us into the presence of the Holy God is anathema to him. This enemy seeks to undermine all that speaks healing and peace to our souls. This enemy would celebrate a culture that concludes a song is worth less than a dollar when in fact it is of immeasurable value.

You may totally agree with me. You may think I am overreacting.

But whether you agree with me or not, at the very least let me simply suggest this. When everyone runs headlong in one direction, it is always a good idea in my opinion to hang back for a minute and ask, "Is there a downside to this?" In this case it may be subtle. But I believe the message that music and songs are worthless is a potentially dangerous one for three reasons:

First, because it may affect the credibility that people give to the song as a form of communication. Since, as we have already seen, a song speaks to both mind and heart and engages the whole brain, its effectiveness is a gift from God.

Second, because in a world where attention spans are increasingly diminishing, it suggests that songs are not worth our time. "Something within us needs what music can give over time," say

Don and Emily Saliers in their book *A Song to Sing, A Life to Live.*
"This kind of deep entering into the moment can be redemptive."[9]
I believe they are correct.

Third, once the ability for people to make any living whatsoever
from writing songs is taken away, gifted writers lose the incentive
to invest in songwriting no matter how deeply they might want to.
After all, they have families to support as well. This means that a lot
of songs that would have been created might never be written. We
hear about antibiotics that may never be discovered because of the
many species of plants lost to rainforest deforestation. In the same
way we may never know what next "Amazing Grace" we have lost
because talented, inspired writers were forced to abandon writing
for economic reasons.

Designed to Respond to Music

I've talked a lot in this book about what music makes us feel and
the ways God can and does use music and songs to communicate
deep universal truths. Science—also a gift from God—and physi-
ology can explain some of this. But in his book *Music, The Brain,
and Ecstasy*, author Robert Jourdain says, "The deeper levels of
understanding at which music seems so 'meaningful' are the least
distinctly mapped."[10] I can't help but wonder if this is because there
are mysteries to music that science will never be able to uncover.
God, after all, is too big to understand, and I believe it is likely that
parts of His creation of the human being will always elude even the
most-skilled scientists.

But for a moment, let's look at a few key things that we do
know. As we learn more and more about the brain, it turns out that
some of it *can* actually be explained using science.

The brain has two hemispheres. Language is processed primarily in the left hemisphere.[11] Melody and harmony are processed primarily in the right auditory cortex, located in the right

hemisphere.[12] Both the left and right sides are necessary for complete perception of rhythm.[13] A song, therefore, containing language, melody, and rhythm engages *the whole brain.* I believe this is what people mean when they say that a song touches both mind and heart. In this case, "mind and heart" is a loosely translated layman's term for the integration that is happening in the different regions of the human brain when a song is being heard.

Therapists who use Music for the Soul's work tell me that because traumatic memories are stored primarily in the right hemisphere of the brain,[14] a song—with its melody and harmony—can be especially helpful in helping unlock painful memories.

In a letter to me, Christian counselor Vicky Kepler Didato writes, "I became fascinated that the medium of music could so quickly tap into what took traditional left brain talk therapy weeks—or months—to get to. I began to research right brain techniques in working with trauma and completely altered the way I had been counseling." The songs "spoke directly to the hearts and souls of victims of trauma and their emotional pain."

This is no accident. It is the way God has made us.

Levitin puts it this way: "Our body is designed to respond to music. It does so without any control or volition on our part. The brain's reward center responds to music. Music changes our state of mind and studies show that it can actually physically change our brain"[15]

Here's another interesting fact. Because, as we have already discussed, vibrations cause sound, it is these vibrations that stimulate your eardrum. When so stimulated your eardrum actually moves in response to the vibrations. So when you say you are "moved" by a song, you aren't kidding.

Neuroscientists such as the late Dr. Oliver Sacks of Columbia University and Dr. Robert J. Zatorre of Montreal Neurological Institute[16] have both done work showing the responsiveness to music in neurologically challenged patients. If music can help stroke patients to speak and Parkinson's patients to walk, both functions of brain response—and if, as Levitin says, "The part of the brain where music goes to directly [is] related to your deep emotions"—it follows then that music can have a profound impact on emotional healing. According to Diane Austin, adjunct associate professor of music therapy at New York University and executive director of the Music Psychotherapy Center in New York, "Nothing accesses the inner world of feelings, sensations, memories, and associations as directly as music does."[17]

Why a song?

Because, after thirty years of seeing God's transforming power at work in music up close and personally in hundreds and hundreds of lives, I believe she is right.

> Music can have a profound impact on emotional healing.

7

MORE BEAUTIFUL

*"Music expresses that which cannot be said
and on which it is impossible to be silent."*
VICTOR HUGO

When Music for the Soul was finally incorporated in December 2001, we had a small but mighty board of directors. They included Lynne McCleery, the woman for whom I'd written at Score Productions; Dr. Doris Sanford, originator of the Hurts of Childhood Series and author of *I Can't Talk about It*; and Marty Wheeler, who had been my song-plugger during my first two Christian music publishing deals with Starsong and McSpadden-Smith.

This was a circle of very special friends who had helped me along my career path in a variety of ways. Collectively they brought a diversity of wisdom and experience as well as each understanding the power of music.

Not long after Music for the Soul was incorporated, the board decided that the first project the ministry should embark on would be a grief project. The reason was simple. Everybody deals with grief at some point in life. It was felt that such a project would have the best chance of resonating with the most number of listeners. As it happens, it would not be until ten years later that we finally released the grief project, *Drink Deep: A Musical Journey through*

Grief as our eleventh full-length CD. This is because a dramatic set of circumstances completely changed our plans.

One morning Marty told me over breakfast that his wife Sandy had been diagnosed with breast cancer. This was particularly devastating because Sandy, only thirty, was seven months pregnant with their first child.

A few days later I was driving to a meeting and listening to music on the car stereo. Suddenly the phrase "No one has ever been more beautiful to me," landed in my head as a complete thought. Clearly, my subconscious was thinking about my friend's situation. Immediately I exclaimed out loud, "Oh my gosh! That is for Marty and Sandy!"

I shut off the music and rummaged for a piece of paper in the glove box, finding an old receipt. The song was coming quickly, and I scribbled furiously. It felt almost like dictation. In less than ten minutes, the melody and the lyric were complete, all of "More Beautiful" written in a moving car.

Though my intent in writing the song was to serve my friends, I was more than a little uncomfortable. It felt so presumptuous. I wanted to share the song with Marty, but I didn't want to offend him. Who was I to assume that I knew what he and Sandy were feeling?

A few evenings later a prayer gathering was held at the home of Shawn McSpadden, our mutual friend. At one point I pulled Marty aside and gave him a tape of the song. I remember saying, "This just came to me. I hope it's a blessing. If it's not, throw it in the trash, and we never need to speak of it again." I know that sounds melodramatic, but I wanted him to feel no pressure whatsoever to respond to what I had written.

The next day I received a lovely message from Marty on my answering machine. He expressed deep appreciation and gratitude for the song. "You gave me exactly the words that I've been wanting to say to Sandy," he said.

The next time we saw each other in person, Marty told me he wasn't going to play the song for Sandy just yet but that he knew there would come a time when she would need to hear the message. "I'm going to save it because I know Sandy is going to hit a place where she will need to know that I think she's beautiful."

The Wheeler's baby girl Hannah was born by C-section five weeks before Sandy's due date. Mother and child appear in a breathtaking photo on the cover of *More Beautiful*. The photo was taken by Marty.

A Good Music for the Soul Project

From there "More Beautiful" seemed to come to life almost on its own. First I created a recording of the song so Marty would have a way to share the song with Sandy.

"I absolutely knew there was going to be a moment where I would need to tell her how beautiful she was to me," Marty said.

One night, after Sandy had been undergoing treatment for some time, the moment came.

"My wife was pretty beat up about losing her hair. We had actually gone and shaved her head and she was bald. I'd had my head shaved as well. She broke down and started crying. She started communicating to me how horrible she felt and how ugly she felt. She actually said, 'I feel like a monster.'"

It was then that Marty told her, "I've got something I want you to hear." He got the CD and played it.

> Now I stand helpless and watch you in pain
> I wish I could fix this, make it all go away
> But here is the one thing that you must believe
> No one was ever more beautiful to me
> No one could ever be more beautiful to me[1]

Marty was able to let Sandy know that he loved her more than ever. "It was a moment of healing. 'More Beautiful' helped me to say what I wanted to say to my wife."*

In my mind, when the idea for Music for the Soul was coming together, I was thinking of serving the needs of listeners who were *out there.* I'd never even considered how God would move in the lives of those who were working with us. Yet here the chairperson of our board was the first person moved by the mission of our ministry. We had barely begun, but my prayers were already being answered. The ministry was already making a difference.

> "I've got something I want you to hear."

Marty suggested to me that if he had found something like this he would have been happy to pay for it and he thought it would make the basis for a good Music for the Soul project. We took Marty's suggestion, and *More Beautiful* became the first Music for the Soul project, reassuring women that breast cancer could not rob them of their true beauty and modeling for husbands and families the importance of a supportive and loving response.

I remember the day the first copies of *More Beautiful* arrived at our house.

Our basement was serving as the ministry office at that time, and I brought one of the boxes inside to open it. When I took Music for the Soul's first CD out and held it in my hand, I dropped into a chair and, out of the blue, began to weep. I couldn't pinpoint why exactly. I suppose some of the tears were tears of relief and some were tears of joy. And some of them were probably tears of gratitude that the seed planted at the conference in New Jersey, thirteen years earlier, had finally broken through the soil.

---

* Sandy Wheeler has now been in remission for several years.

After the CD was released, we heard from breast cancer survivors all around the country.

Beverly in Washington, DC, said, "As a breast cancer survivor, I can tell you that the song 'More Beautiful' brought comfort and healing to me and my family and to the many cancer survivors who are my patients. When I listen to the song a great weight is lifted off my shoulders. I can actually feel it happening."

> God knows the heart of every listener intimately.

Julie, a breast cancer survivor from Michigan, reached out and shared, "I am a breast cancer survivor. I have counseled many women with breast cancer across the United States since my diagnosis in 2004. I have talked to husbands as well." She told us she planned to put the CD in the hands of every husband of a woman with breast cancer. "It is perfect," she said.

When someone is going through a personal crisis, it can have the effect of being very isolating. People can feel alone, as if no one could possibly understand what they and the ones they love are going through.

The thought that the song "More Beautiful" was going to help other husbands have words of comfort and support for their hurting wives was an affirmation. Music for the Soul was going to be able to speak, through song, into those hurting places and help people feel understood and consoled.

What was truly amazing was the way we almost immediately saw God take the song "out of context."

One woman shared that she had been through a miscarriage. "Only weeks after we found out that we were pregnant, I had to go into emergency surgery to have the remains of my baby removed. It's been a hard couple of months. But, my husband keeps telling me that I'm more beautiful than ever. Thank you for your song. It brought home exactly what he was trying to tell me."

Another woman living in Canyon Country, California—a very warm part of the country—shared that ever since having neck surgery she'd been wearing turtleneck sweaters to hide the resulting scar. "After hearing 'More Beautiful' I threw my turtlenecks away."

Responses like these forever changed the way I pray before writing issue-oriented songs. I now understand that if there are five hundred different people listening to a song then there are five hundred different songs being heard. Why?

We all have memories and life experiences that shape the way we see the world. When we listen to a song, it elicits a response from us based not only on what the song is actually saying but also on the way we are interpreting the lyric and music because of what we've been through. The overlay of our life's journey provides an individualized context for the song.

I trust God knows the heart of every listener intimately and can choose, through the Holy Spirit, to use the song and make it meaningful to all kinds of people in all kinds of situations.

Though "More Beautiful" was created with one specific situation in mind, God used it to accomplish His own purpose in the individual hearts of the woman who had miscarried and the woman who had neck surgery. The fact that in each of those cases the context was completely different than the one I had in mind while writing the song doesn't matter. It is God who knows every person's story and who knows what every listener needs to hear in order to receive the healing he or she needs.

We may never know who will be at the other end of a song we write and record. As such, I now pray that God will guide us in the process to create something that can serve and accomplish the purpose God has in mind for each individual listener. And I pray for a blessing to take place in the heart of every person who hears the song.

A Dream Comes to Life

Speaking of what is needed, I was very surprised a little less than two years later when the *More Beautiful* project took a turn that I never could have anticipated.

One afternoon—again driving in my car!—I received a call from my friend Corey Niemchick. Corey is cofounder and president of Storytelling Pictures, an award-winning documentary film company in Grand Rapids, Michigan.

I had first heard from Corey several years earlier when he was a Christian recording artist. He had recorded a song I wrote with Scott Krippayne entitled "All of My Hope Is in You." He'd reached out to share with me the responses he was getting from his audiences when he played the song. In particular he wanted to tell me about the encouragement it had given to one family whose son was struggling with a brain tumor. I had come to know Corey as a man with a tender, compassionate heart, and by this time we had written many songs together.

On this occasion he called because he had an idea for a new song and a music video for our "More Beautiful" piece. He proceeded to tell me about a dream that a member of his church named Lynda Plowman had shared with him.

Lynda was in a struggle with breast cancer. In her dream Lynda saw herself going to an amusement park with her family. As they approached the roller-coaster ride, the attendants would not let her family get on the ride with her. She had to ride alone. As the coaster came back around to the end of the ride, it slowed down but it didn't stop. As she tried to reach out to her family, the ride sped up again—and she had to take the ride over and over and over again . . . each time, alone.

After having this dream several nights, Lynda realized that this was a metaphor for her struggle with cancer. As Corey and his business partner at Storytelling Pictures, John Evans, were talking about Lynda's remarkable dream, a vision began to emerge that sharing this story in a video might be a very powerful way to help others in the same situation.

Corey asked me if I thought we could write a song about Lynda's story. It wasn't long before Corey and I were sitting in the Music for the Soul Nashville office working on what would become the song "The Wildest Ride on Earth."

It was just an ordinary day
Then in a moment everything had changed.
Out of the familiar—into the unknown.
I close my eyes, hold my breath
Caught between life and death
I'm gonna have to take this ride alone.

The bar comes down
I'm hanging on
The panic starts to rise
A twist—a turn, the bottom drops
I'm fighting for my life.
My heart pounds, can't catch my breath
And everything's a blur
No one wants a ticket
for the wildest ride on earth[2]

We completed the song; and thanks to Lynda's courage, the support of her family, and the incredible creativity of Corey, John, and the entire Storytelling Pictures team, the music video became a reality. In addition, there were some inspiring interview pieces and some behind-the-scenes documentary footage.

The filming of the music video itself took place at a theme park in Michigan on a very chilly night. Cameras were positioned on and around a giant wooden roller coaster. Actress Lauren Theil, who had her head shaved in preparation for the lead role, was wearing nothing but a blue hospital gown. She had to ride the violent coaster multiple times in order for the crew to capture the needed footage. She was so uncomfortable that during one break in the action she said, "I can't do this anymore."

Lynda, who was present for the filming, put her arm around Lauren to encourage her and gently but firmly said, "You can't quit because I couldn't."

Weeks later I sat in the Storytelling Pictures office to view the completed music video for the first time. It was overwhelming—one of the most incredibly humbling experiences of my life. I remember thinking, *God, why am I blessed to be the one who gets to share this with the world?* Once again, God had taken a song written in response to the pain of a friend, as with "We're All in This Together," and expanded it into something beyond anything I could have ever imagined.

This feeling only increased as the award-winning video generated incredible responses. Perhaps the one that moved me most deeply was that of Georgia Shaffer, a Pennsylvania psychologist, author, and breast cancer survivor. She told me that after having dealt with her cancer for eighteen years she didn't think she had any tears left to cry. But she said when she watched "the music video *Wildest Ride on Earth,* I was touched so profoundly I just sobbed. Although my tears were rooted in the painful experience of battling cancer for years, the result was a healing deep in my soul." Georgia told me that in her opinion, the *More Beautiful* project came from the hand of God. For me this was a powerful affirmation of the ability of the arts to be able to communicate healing to the most private places in our hearts.

Time and again women have shared how aptly the roller-coaster analogy captures the breast cancer experience. I'm so glad that

Lynda, Sandy, and Marty so unselfishly shared their stories. It's amazing how, when we are willing to be vulnerable, God will use our story to bless someone else.

Songs from More Beautiful *can be streamed at* www.musicforthesoul.org/resources/more-beautiful.

8

Whole in the Sight of God

*"After silence, that which comes nearest
to expressing the inexpressible is music."*
ALDOUS HUXLEY

In the fourth month of my wife's second pregnancy, we went in for her to have a routine ultrasound. During the procedure we heard the words no one ever wants to hear in a doctor's office.

"I hate to be the one to tell you this."

The baby my wife Meredith was carrying had an opening at the base of the spine. I asked the technician whether the child was a girl or a boy. "You want to know?" she asked, seemingly perplexed that I would want the information. My thought was we would need to know the sex of the baby to be able to name and pray for the child. That's how we found out we had a son who was in trouble.

Later that day we were ushered into the office of a specialist who told us that our son had a condition called spina bifida. He said our son was going to be very sick and that we should seriously consider terminating the pregnancy. He told us we had a week to decide.

Up until then, abortion had always been an abstract concept for us, existing only as a point of conversation. Accordingly, I'd had an intellectual perspective. Now it was an issue of our own flesh and blood. Everybody in our extended family had an opinion. It wasn't long before the pressure started from *both* sides, and the situation threatened to become quickly divisive.

My wife and I, not wanting to pressure each other, decided we would pray separately for the week and then come back together, make our joint decision, and only then share it with our family and friends.

We were living in a new city and had no permanent church home. I called Rev. Larry Keene, the pastor of the church we'd attended for the past ten years in California, and told him the news.

He told me that his experience was that "special needs children were compensated in the spirit." He said the church would be praying for us.

We had one of those miniature churches with the lighted windows that go underneath the Christmas tree every year. I got that out and plugged it in and placed it on top of our bedroom dresser, so when we awakened on those first fitful nights after we got the news, we could see that little church and remember our church family back in Los Angeles was praying for us.

One morning I got up very early and stood by the dining room window. As I watched the sun come up, I saw a robin alight in the dogwood tree in our front yard. As I thought about my son, I realized, "He'll be able to hear a bird sing. He'll be able to watch the sunrise. He'll be able to laugh. He'll be able to give and receive love."

In that moment I realized that God was not sending us a body to care for but a soul.

Later, as I was praying, I found myself thinking about my wife and daughter. I thought, *If one of them was in a car accident and*

I was told they would never be able to walk again, I wouldn't tell the doctors to put them to sleep. I found myself realizing that all of us are broken in one way or another and yet God loves us.

I drove over to Starsong and sequestered myself away in a small writer's room with exposed plumbing, a folding chair, and a piano. There I felt God minister to me as I wrote these words:

> *Johnny sits in his wheelchair as the children run and play*
> *Feeling the warm summer sun upon his face*
> *He moves everyone with his laughter and light*
> *and through prayers they lift up for him every night*
>
> *He is whole in the sight of God*
> *He is whole in the sight of God*
> *He can run to all things on the path of the spirit*
> *He is whole in the sight of God*[1]

When Meredith and I came together at the end of that week, we had arrived at the same decision.

Once the doctors at Vanderbilt knew we were moving forward with the pregnancy, they offered us a first-of-its-kind intrauterine surgery to repair our son's spine. I wanted to do it. My wife wasn't sure. She felt like our son was safe in the womb. I wanted to do whatever we could to try and fix the problem.

We decided to go ahead with the surgery but pray that God would stop it if we were making the wrong decision. When we went in for another ultrasound, the doctor told us he was sorry, but the placenta had moved into a position that made the surgery impossible.

We had our answer.

As it turns out, my wife's uncle was a friend of a doctor who, at that time, ran a spina bifida clinic in Chicago. When we contacted him and told him what we'd been through, he said, "I'm glad you didn't have the surgery." He felt the womb was a safe environment and wouldn't cause any further damage. It was a grace-filled affirmation.

It's a Song that Rescues You

Henry had emergency neurosurgery the day he was born and spent the first several hours of his life in intensive care. There were several anxious moments during the next few weeks as we monitored his recovery. The next four years of his life were full of more surgeries, casts, and doctors' appointments. It was hard on him and hard on our family.

My wife and I did our best to insulate our daughter Stephanie from the pain Henry's condition caused her mother and me. Accordingly, Stephanie always seemed to handle Henry's situation well, accepting it as normal. She was an attentive sister who played often with her brother laughing easily and often.

We even commented to each other about "how well" Stephanie was doing. Her brother's situation didn't seem to be affecting her negatively—or so we thought.

On Wednesday nights Stephanie and I went to a weekly dinner and program at our church called Fellowfest. It was a dedicated daddy/daughter time that we both looked forward to eagerly.

One night on the way home from Fellowfest I popped a new CD into the player in our car. It was a record I had just finished producing and included a song I had written several years earlier called "The Lord Sent a Child."

When we were about five minutes from home, the song started playing. A waltz with acoustic guitar, orchestra, and vocal, it was not the kind of arrangement that one would normally expect to captivate a seven-year-old.

Stephanie had been perky all evening, even for the first several minutes of the ride home. But as the song progressed, she began to retreat into herself, and I saw a gathering cloud come over her face.

We arrived home, and I pulled the car around to the back of our house underneath the carport and shut off the engine. I looked over at Stephanie who was clearly distressed and very quiet. Something told me not to speak.

> A song can be the device that opens up the heart.

Then suddenly she lunged at me, threw her arms around my neck, and cried out, "My brother! His legs!!" immediately dissolving into sobs.

We sat there for several minutes, and I just held her as she cried out all the pain that she had been holding inside. A song I had written about the Christ child before my own children were born had been able to speak to a deep place in my daughter's heart that needed to let go.

I have since come to believe that a song can be the device that opens up the heart and reveals where healing needs to take place. At times a song can even be a lifeline, reaching a closed heart when nothing else will.

Christian songwriting legend Gloria Gaither says, "A sermon won't do it. A book won't do it. When you're going down for the third time, it's a song that rescues you."

But just like someone who has been rescued from a perilous physical situation is taken to a doctor to be checked out, someone who has an emotional breakthrough should also go and speak with a professional.

In retrospect I wish we had taken our daughter to speak with a therapist at the time to give her the tools to better process the feelings she was experiencing. She had been through a very traumatic situation, and she could, as could we all, have benefited from the opportunity to speak with a counselor about what our family had been through.

Healing through Creating

It was a few years later when I felt led to share the song "Whole in the Sight of God" through Music for the Soul on a project for families loving a child with special needs. I envisioned a full orchestra accompanying a pianist and a tenor vocalist. Such an approach called for a very special arrangement.

I'd had the opportunity to work and become friends with a phenomenally talented music arranger named Phillip Keveren.[2] I asked Phillip if he would write an orchestra arrangement for "Whole in the Sight of God." He agreed, and what he told me after the recording was completed absolutely floored me.

Phillip grew up in a small town in eastern Oregon. He had two brothers, one older and one younger. As it so happens, the older of the two brothers, David, was born with a spinal condition. This was in the 1970s before doctors were able to do the type of surgery that saved my son's life.

When he was a boy, Phillip's mother made several trips to the city to take his brother David to the hospital, often staying for several days at a time. This caused Phillip to resent his brother for taking so much of his mother's time away from him. Subsequently, when David died, Phillip felt a tremendous sense of guilt over having had such negative thoughts and feelings about his brother.

Phillip shared that all throughout the years he had never talked about any of this with his mother. The process of arranging the song "Whole in the Sight of God" had caused him to reflect on how he experienced his brother's situation as a young boy. Now a father of two himself, from the vantage point of adulthood, he was able to see and appreciate what his mother had done in order to care for his brother.

Phillip was able to reach out to his mother and talk openly about how he felt as a child and heal this area of their relationship. In the process of preparing "Whole in the Sight of God" to be recorded, God had, once again, used our desire to serve others to minister to a member of our own team.

When the time came to record the vocal for the song, I knew I wanted someone who would bring his or her whole heart to the performance and be willing to be vulnerable to the lyric. I could imagine only one person singing it, and that was Scott Krippayne.

In Nashville the professional singers who work in the recording studios are so talented they sound great even when they aren't really putting their heart into it. Studio singer extraordinaire Felicia Farerre calls this "renting to own."

But there is another gear that the truly great ones have. It is the ability to inhabit a lyric and bring their whole heart to what it is that they're singing. Then, not only does it sound great, but you can actually feel the difference.

Scott Krippayne inhabits a vocal. He takes each word of a lyric and squeezes every available ounce of heart and soul out of it. In addition to having a stellar tenor voice and a tender heart, Scott is also a dad. I knew he was the perfect choice for the song.

Scott agreed to sing the song, and one morning a few weeks later we got together at Kent Hooper's House of Big studio to record the vocal. Everything went fine until we got to the last verse. It goes like this:

> *Katie lives deep in silence where music never plays*
> *Finding her songs in the joys of each new day*
> *Without notes she's creating a new symphony*
> *'Cause her gentle sweet soul is its own melody*
> *She is whole in the sight of God*
> *She is whole in the sight of God*
> *She can hear all things through the words of the Spirit*
> *She is whole in the sight of God*

Scott could not get through it. He broke down in tears. He told me later that in the process of trying to sing the song he had become deeply aware of how much the gift of music means to him. The idea of someone being deaf and never getting to experience what brings him such profound joy had broken Scott's heart to the point where he literally couldn't get the words to come out.

I almost wished I could have left it that way on the final recording. It had been a moment when the song had touched the singer at a place beyond words—when only tears could express the emotions overwhelming his heart.

> The song had touched the singer at a place beyond words.

I'm confident that people hear this in the final recording. Scott's vulnerability invites those listening who are caring for and loving someone with special needs to feel embraced and encouraged.

I can tell you from personal experience that having a child with special needs in your home can be isolating. In some ways, you want it to be. Lots of what must be attended to feels quite personal, and there is a desire to respect the privacy of your loved one. At the same time there is also a desire to not be an object of pity for others.

And yet there is that side of all of us that wants to be able to share what we are going through with others and feel understood. Often, even in church, people said, "Henry is doing so well. It's just a miracle!" Of course they meant well, but they were putting the happy face on the situation that made them comfortable, not asking us what we might actually be feeling.

That was when my wife verbalized the distinction that most people were not "safe" to speak with regarding how Henry's special needs affected our family. Accordingly we became very selective about who we shared with, choosing people who were able to be understanding and supportive of our situation.

One of the most cherished responses we've ever received to a Music for the Soul song came from somebody whom I knew understood these kinds of feelings well. It occurred only a few months after "Whole in the Sight of God" was released. It was a phone call from a woman named Erika. She told me that she and her husband were in their seventies and that he was now in a nearly vegetative state, requiring constant attention. They were on a fixed income, and she was not able to hire outside help. She said that was really OK with her because she wanted to be able to preserve his dignity.

Then she said, "Sometimes you don't want other people around, but you still want to feel like somebody understands. Listening to 'Whole in the Sight of God' is like having a support group here. I cried all morning pouring my heart out to God. God speaks through this."

She asked some questions about the ministry and encouraged me to keep doing what we were doing. I thanked her, and before ending the call we prayed together.

A few days later an envelope came in the mail. Inside was a note from Erika thanking me and apologizing because she couldn't do more to support us. Inside were two crumpled one-dollar bills. Immediately the story of the widow's offering from Mark 12:40–44 came to mind.

I have felt blessed in ministry on many occasions but never more so than on that day.

A Crooked Road

"Why did God make me this way?"

I knew the question would eventually come, and I'd prayed about how I would answer it. Henry was seven years old when he finally asked me that question one evening as I was helping him with some spina bifida-related activities. I gave him the only answer I could think of that was not a lie.

"I don't know, son."

Oh, of course I could've gone into some theological rationalization and told him all about how God was going to use his infirmity to bless others; how truthfully, in fact, He already had—as hundreds of people had prayed for Henry for the weeks and months leading up to his birth and through the four years of surgeries that had followed.

Somehow, though, I didn't think that would bring him much comfort. So I decided to sit with him in the question. I decided not to minimize his pain. I decided not to explain away his condition by making it a part of some gigantic cosmic puzzle that God was working.

I've come to believe that we who call ourselves Christians are too quick to come up with explanations at times like these. I've come to believe that we do not place enough value in the ministry of presence, of simply being there with someone. There is something holy that happens when we are willing to be still in the company of another human being and let God's presence fill the space.

What I do know for sure is that God loves us, cherishes us. I know God is present with us on every mountaintop and in every valley. I believe that God is constantly at work reconciling, redeeming, and working in and through us to make something beautiful out of the challenges in our lives.

I even believe that sometimes God heals miraculously. I can't explain it, and quite frankly, I don't feel the need to. It's not my call to make.

Many who prayed for our son before he was born prayed for a total healing. Some told us that if we prayed hard enough and prayed the right things that he'd be healed. To harbor any doubt would show a lack of faith and result in our son not being healed.

Now any parent will tell you that he'd dress like Bozo the clown and eat Brussels sprouts three meals a day for the rest of his life if it meant his child would be healed. But to add to the almost unendurable road of walking with a severely ill child the potential

for guilt by suggesting to parents that God would withhold healing if they didn't pray correctly? Well, that's just plain cruel and leaves no room for grace.

Ultimately we prayed for healing but also prayed that if he were not to be healed we'd have the courage to handle whatever came. Meanwhile, the doctors warned us that Henry would most likely not be able to walk and would probably develop hydrocephalus, a condition in which fluid accumulates on the brain, and need a shunt.

> God is not afraid of our questions.

I still remember our joy the day Henry pulled himself up— incredibly with casts on *both* legs—and took his first steps! I also remember our immense relief when he did *not* develop hydrocephalus.

Many of the parents at the clinic where we took our son had children who experienced vastly different outcomes, most not doing nearly as well as Henry. Is that because we prayed more rightly than they? Is that because we loved our child more than they loved theirs? Or that *God* loved our child more? I don't believe any of those things.

What I do believe is that God hears prayer. What I do believe is that God desires relationship with us. And what I believe most of all is that God is not afraid of our questions and even our anger when we have to walk a crooked road.

A song can be a great place to examine difficult questions like these. As was noted in chapter 6, the best songs make us *feel* a thought. But writing these kinds of songs requires a kind of transparency and honesty that, while cathartic, can also be frightening as the writer bears their soul to the world.

When teaching co-writing at Christian songwriting seminars such as Write About Jesus, I use a graphic analogy to express this vulnerability: "You have to be willing to rip your chest open, throw your heart out on the table, and let other people stomp around in it. If you're not willing to be that open, you'll never get to anything that anybody really needs to hear."

If those who create music, or any other kind of art, are willing to be this honest, then they may find that they are deeply ministered to themselves in the process of creating something that will ultimately minister to others.

In 2010 I became aware of a young man named Christopher Bailey who was living with juvenile diabetes. A gifted author at the age of sixteen, he had written profoundly and with moving honesty about trying to reconcile the anger and frustration he felt over his disease with his belief in a loving God.

Together we created a song in hopes of expressing his feelings in a way that would help others living with a chronic disease know they are not alone.

> *If You love me, God*
> *Why did You let this happen?*
> *Are You in this place*
> *I could not have imagined?*
> *I'm crying out for peace*
> *And the patience that comes from You alone*
> *Lord, give me faith to walk this crooked road*[3]

In addition to being helpful for the listener, this kind of creativity can help the writer by giving vent to the inner turmoil and mental struggles that come with the burden of a chronic disease.

This cathartic process offers the potential for emotional healing to take place. Also, this kind of wrestling with God, rather than diminishing our faith, can bring us into a deeper, richer, and more truthful relationship.

The truth is that all of us are walking a crooked road in one way or another. And all of us are whole in the sight of the God who created us and looks past our individual brokenness to the soul He has placed within us.

That God, who loves us well beyond anything we can imagine, is *always* with us.

Songs from Whole in the Sight of God *can be streamed at www.musicforthesoul.org/resources/whole-in-the-sight-of-god.*

"Crooked Road" can be streamed at www.musicforthesoul.org/resources/crooked-road.

HORIZONTAL WORSHIP

"'Love the Lord your God with all your heart
and with all your soul and with all your mind.'
This is the first and greatest commandment.
And the second is like it: 'Love your neighbor as yourself.'"
JESUS CHRIST, MATTHEW 22:37–39

We live in a world full of broken, hurting people. This includes all of us. Everybody is having a hard life. Even the person you envy the most has experienced—or will experience—deep pain.

Another way of saying this is that everyone has a story. Songs are one of the ways we tell those stories.

Roughly twenty-five years ago, what is now commonly referred to as contemporary praise and worship music began a rapid rise to popularity, transforming the musical content in the worship services of many congregations.

I'm not going to spend any time arguing the relative merits of praise and worship songs versus the older, traditional hymns. This silly war has divided way too many churches, embroiling them in a style-over-substance, robes-versus-rock-bands debate that subjugates the importance of community.

What concerns me far more about the praise and worship songs in our contemporary services is not what they are but what they are not.

The lyrics of the vast majority of praise and worship choruses celebrate the greatness of God, usually in the person of Jesus Christ. They tell us that God (or Jesus) is awesome, powerful, and worthy of praise. They lift Him on high, behold Him in glory, and crown Him Lord and King of all.

> We love Christ through how we love one another.

In short, they are vertical in focus, sung to the object of our worship. Insofar as they go, they successfully accomplish what it is they are trying to do.

So, what's the problem?

They only tell *half* of the story.

In the "greatest commandment," Jesus has instructed us to love God and love our neighbors as ourselves. Current praise and worship accomplishes the first half of this instruction beautifully but routinely disregards the second half.

I know some who would argue that a worship service is for God and as such that all of the music in worship should be a gift to Him. In other words, all of the music in our worship services must be vertical in nature.

But if, as Scripture suggests, we love Christ through how we love one another, it seems then that to fully express our love of God we should express both vertical and horizontal themes in our worship.

I think this idea can best be represented by a triangle. In worship, God's love is flowing down to me and to the person next to me as well. Ideally, adoration and praise are flowing back up to God, both from me and the person beside me. But it is when we are also reaching out toward each other in the spirit of Christ, fulfilling the second part of the Great Commandment that the triangle is completed. The love of God is now flowing down to us, up to God, and between each other.

At the very least, when this happens we will be deepening the fellowship with our brothers and sisters in Christ. At the most, it means that we won't miss an opportunity to live out the Great Commission. Allow me to explain what I mean.

Let's say that Jane and Jim are each going through a terribly difficult time in their lives. Jane's never been to church. Jim went to church for a while several years ago but had a bad experience and hasn't been back in a long, long time. Jane is ashamed about something that happened long ago. This shame has her feeling like God could never love her. Jim feels guilty about the life he's been living and feels like God could never forgive him.

They each finally get up the courage to set foot in a church. The service begins, with twenty to thirty minutes of praise and worship music.

Jane isn't familiar with church lingo. How does singing the average contemporary worship song speak to the person who has no relationship with God? Praise comes out of a heart overflowing with gratefulness after experiencing God's goodness and love in one's own life. For a nonbeliever then, these songs speak a foreign language. "Worthy is the lamb," doesn't mean anything to Jane.

Jim's former church experience left him feeling that God was distant, judgmental, or indifferent. People all around are lifting their hands in the air, apparently responding to something in the song, but Jim doesn't know what it is because the song isn't speaking to him. He is finding the song to be at best full of platitudes and wishful thinking or at worst a series of outright lies. In any event, for Jim, these songs don't reflect his lived experience of God or the church.

They both begin to get the general gist of the lyrics. Jane hears that God is great and awesome and powerful. She feels more certain than ever that such a God could never love someone as shameful as she is. Jim is pretty sure that this high and mighty God he is hearing about is not going to go down into the pit where he's been hanging out.

Maybe Jane and Jim sing along; maybe they don't. Maybe they stay for the sermon; maybe they don't. The point is this. An opportunity has been missed.

And this is true not only for the visitors. Church members and other regular worship attendees may believe in God, love God, and desire to praise God. But if they are suffering in silence—whether from abuse, addiction, family problems, money issues, disease, or guilt and shame from who knows what else—praising God may be painful, difficult, or just downright impossible.

But what if during the worship time, one or two of these song slots had been used to reach *out* instead of to reach *up*.

When Jesus was on the cross suffering unimaginable pain, His arms were reaching out not only to the thieves on each side of Him but to each of us, as if to say, "I understand your pain, and I love you enough to share it with you." Just as Jesus' arms were spread open for all, welcoming each one of us in the single greatest act of forgiveness in history, the arms of the singing congregation can be spread wide open in song. That's the song that allows us to reach out across the aisle and say, "God loves you and cares about you, and so do I." It's the song that says, "You are not alone. Christ is with you right where you are." It's the song that says, "No one here is looking down on you. We all need grace."

Honoring One Another's Stories

This is the call upon all of us as Christians: to notice those on our left and right and to love them with the compassion of Christ. We cannot do this by looking only vertically. And we certainly cannot do it by living our lives parallel to one another, walking in a self-serving straight line.

To approach worship in a vertical-only manner, then, can be antithetical to the intended purpose of loving God and neighbor as ourselves when it insulates us from the concerns of those around us.

And there is no need to do that because here is the thing. A song can be both vertical and horizontal in its message. An old African-American spiritual demonstrates this with simple beauty and power:

Nobody knows the trouble I've seen
Nobody knows but Jesus
Nobody knows the trouble I've seen
Glory hallelujah

In just a few lines we have acknowledged the omniscience of Christ and the fact that our lives are almost too difficult for words.

All of us have those stories that are hard to tell, but God knows those stories. When our brokenness and our mistakes and our failures are all we have to give God, then that *IS* our gift to Him. Though such a song may seem horizontal on the surface, a song that shares the truth of where we are in our lives becomes God-honoring and vertical by virtue of its honesty. Such a song can easily be just as worshipful as a song with lyrics that only express feelings in positive terms of admiration.

And the singing of songs that let us know that God loves us even though He knows our darkest secrets can be restorative and healing to our spirit. They can give vent to the burdens we carry, lifting them from our shoulders even as we sing the words. Songs like this can create in us a deep longing for a closer relationship with the God who understands and cares about what we are going through.

Presbyterian minister Rev. Stacy Rector says, "There is no pit so low or fire so hot that God will not move heaven and earth to share it with us." Songs that express our deepest hurts, then, open the door for the compassion of Christ to be experienced.

In creating this opportunity, we honor each other's stories without even having to know the details. Someone who might otherwise leave a worship service feeling like nothing in the songs spoke to anything going on in his or her life, might instead leave the service with assurance of God's grace, forgiveness, and love.

With horizontal themes in our music, we also have the potential to change the tone of worship in a way that affects the hearts of the congregation, making each of us more mindful of the pain of those around us. This can have a carryover effect when the music stops. After all, worship is not the only time in a church setting when someone should experience the compassion of Christ. Each one of us, as a follower of Christ's example, should be thinking about ways to make that compassion real for those in our faith community—and beyond!

Every Heart in the Room

For those who might still doubt the value of horizontal songs in a worship setting, consider this question: When in your life have you felt closest to God? Has it been in the times when everything was going your way? Or has it been in the times when you felt like you were at the end of your rope and didn't know what to do or where to turn?

If, like me, your answer is the latter, then why wouldn't we want to include songs in our worship that offer the opportunity for the greatest sense of God's closeness?

Against the backdrop of this conversation I want to share one of the most profound worship experiences of my entire life.

In late 2006, a Bible study book entitled *The Call to Follow Christ*[1] was released. It included a companion CD featuring seven songs recorded by Damaris Carbaugh. I had been a co-writer on these songs with Scott Krippayne and the legendary Tony Wood.

The following summer I received an e-mail from my friend Cindy Wilt, who had been my song-plugger during my five-year stint as a staff songwriter at Word Music. She volunteered at the women's prison in Nashville and had been leading a group of women in a study of *The Call to Follow Christ*.

The women were about to complete the study, and Cindy was planning a graduation ceremony for them. Because the women had learned several of the songs as a part of going through the study, Cindy wanted to know if Scott, Tony, and I would be willing to perform them live at the graduation ceremony.

When in your life have you felt closest to God?

It helps to understand that of the three of us Scotty is by far the best singer. As I mentioned in the previous chapter, no one on earth pulls more emotion out of a song than Scott Krippayne. He cares, and you can hear that he cares. That's why he is featured as a vocalist on all but one of the Music for the Soul CDs.

So Cindy's invitation presented a problem. By this time Scott, who was a Nashville-based writer for several years, had relocated to Tacoma, Washington. Tony couldn't make it either. So that left me, or no one. Cindy assured me the ladies would be excited no matter which one of us could attend.

The day came, and Cindy and I met in the prison parking lot. Going in through the checkpoints and beyond the fence topped with barbed wire, I felt a vague discomfort. The thought came to mind, *I get to go home when this is over. These women have to* stay *here.* An obvious thought, I know, but still the weight of it settled in on me.

Cindy, the other class leaders, and I were first to arrive at the location for the graduation, a small rectangular room crammed with enough folding chairs to seat about seventy-five people. At the front of the room was a small electric keyboard and microphone along with a stool for me to sit on as I played.

A few moments later the women, dressed in prison blues, filed into the room. The group was ethnically diverse, and most seemed to be between the ages of twenty-five and forty-five.

Cindy led the group in a prayer and some other matters of business before introducing me. I said a few words, thanking them for having me, and then began singing the first song.

Then something remarkable happened. A wave of voices washed over me.

I had been so concerned about whether my singing would be good enough for these ladies, and here they were so busy bursting forth in song that they couldn't even hear me. I was suddenly the accompanist for an outpouring of joy! The smiles on their faces and their total lack of self-consciousness immediately put me at ease as we moved through the songs from the CD.

Then it came time to share a song from the project entitled "I Choose Grace." When I began the song, the room grew very quiet as I went through the first few lines of the verse. Their voices rose again when I got to the chorus:

> I choose grace
> I choose grace
> I won't hold on to anger
> To judge is not my place
> I choose grace
> I choose grace
> When I look into my Savior's face
> I choose grace[2]

As I tried to sing with them, the words got caught in my throat and the tears leapt to my eyes.

I know from others who have served in women's prison ministries that the vast majority of women in prison have been victimized in their life at some point. Many have been abused, some sexually, or have been victims of domestic violence or other forms of assault. Others have grown up in a broken or violent home. Some have suffered all of these injustices.

I grew up in a home where I was unconditionally loved. I have never been hungry or abandoned or abused. I have a loving wife and many more good friends than I deserve. I do what I love for a living.

It is one thing for me to choose grace. For this room full of women, it was quite another.

Their courage in singing these words broke me completely. They sang on as I played on keys wet with tears. When the song was over, I knelt behind the stool and wept as Cindy continued with the service. It was one of the most humbling experiences of my lifetime. I had learned the deep, true meaning of my own song through hearing it sung by these women. Their voices singing those words convicted me in a way that writing the song had not.

I was suddenly profoundly grateful for being the only one of us writers available to sing on this day. When it was time to close the service, the women asked me if we could do the song again. I held it together a little better the second time.

Later, several of the women came up to speak with me personally. A lady named Evangeline said, "Your song has helped me heal." A young woman named Ann said, "I'm trying to forgive what was done to me and it's hard. 'I Choose Grace' is helping." Another lady named Jerri said, "When I hear your song I feel like angels are all around me."

This was a song about being disappointed in myself for the ways I had acted unkindly and thoughtlessly toward others. It was about how I had been changed into someone willing to offer grace to others because of my own experience with God's forgiveness.

This was an "I" song, not a vertical "You" song praising God. But I have never taken part in a more worshipful gathering than with those women on that day.

Each one of the women in the room brought her story with her to that service. In the singing of "I Choose Grace," both vertical and horizontal worship took place. In the singing of that song, God spoke into every heart in the room with His reconciling, healing love. In the singing of that song, the women felt supported, upheld, and understood not only by God but also by one another—simply put, *not alone*. In the singing of the song, not only the women but I, as well, felt humbled by God's inexplicable grace.

And in the singing of that song, God was glorified.

COMFORT IN THE
CHAOS

"Music was my refuge. I could crawl
into the space between the notes and curl my back to loneliness."
MAYA ANGELOU

After a few years as a Nashville-based songwriter, I was invited to be part of a group that critiqued songs submitted to NSAI, short for Nashville Songwriters Association International.

The majority of the songs that we reviewed were on a beginner's level. That was why it was all the more startling when one day I pressed Play and listened to a song called "When My Feet Left the Ground."

The song was about what a person was thinking while falling through the air after jumping off a bridge to commit suicide. The song was superbly written, compelling, and disturbing. I was impressed.

And worried.

Though we were not supposed to contact the writers who submitted the songs, I asked for special permission from the program's director to reach out to the writer because the song was so powerful I actually feared that he might be in danger of taking his own life.

When I connected with the writer, a Quaker named James Yarsky living in New York, I was relieved to discover the song had been an exercise in using his powers of imagination. He was flattered and rather surprised that I'd been concerned about him. We soon became friends, and I had the opportunity to hear many more of James's songs, which I found to be a compelling combination of emotion and intellect. The uncompromising honesty of his songs, coupled with his intense vocal delivery, never failed to elicit a response in me.

God can use people from all backgrounds.

The rawness of his work gave me a whole new appreciation for how a song could be used to speak powerfully and profoundly to the deepest, most-wounded places in a listener. His ability to establish an emotional connection on a topic that was normally out of bounds seemed to open the door to all kinds of possibilities.

I have since come to believe that when dealing with life's toughest issues it is important to write songs that not only mention the pain but actually pitch a tent and camp out in it.

Through the years I have heard many Christian counselors complain about the "just believe in Jesus and everything will be OK" approach that much of the organized church has often taken with regard to serious emotional issues. During my years as a contemporary Christian music writer, I had heard many Christian songs that I felt were guilty of the same thing. Though well meaning, songs like these run the risk of being far too simplistic to resonate with people facing unrelenting agony over issues like addiction, chronic disease, suicide grief, and such. By skimming the surface, I believe songs like these can potentially serve to drive someone away from Christian music and Christianity itself, feeling that it trivializes the very thing with which they are struggling most mightily.

The unvarnished pain that I found in James's songs is more routinely on display in the songs of secular recording artists. While I would not give a blanket endorsement to the catalogs of most pop, rock, hip-hop, or country artists, many times the honesty in their writing and singing is profound and carries with it the potential to be the connection point people need to begin the healing journey.

Just because a song doesn't have a Scripture reference, doesn't mean it can't share a divine truth. God can use people from all backgrounds and all walks of life to speak to us, even if they do not claim any religious affiliation.

In writing a song that means to convey a specific point about the healing process, I will often choose to leave Jesus out of it, depending on the point the song is trying to make. I won't shoehorn Jesus into a song to make someone comfortable.

Don't get me wrong. I believe Jesus is the ultimate key to finding true freedom from any of the ills that befall us. But I also believe that God has given us many important tools that, when used in concert with faith, can help equip a person to achieve the fullest measure of wellness.

I think it is also important to remember that many people carry baggage from unfortunate church experiences early in life. Many automatically put up a wall to block any message they perceive as Christian. A song that resonates with their personal experience without using religious language can often be a way to build a bridge.

I've found that what it comes down to is people won't trust you with their hope unless they believe that you understand their pain. To skip ahead to victory in Jesus without first being the Jesus of Matthew 25 is to potentially short-circuit the healing process. In that passage Jesus says, "For I was hungry and you gave me something to eat, I was thirsty and you gave me something to drink, I was a stranger and you invited me in, I needed clothes and you clothed me, I was sick and you looked after me, I was in prison and you came to visit me" (vv. 35–36).

As John Maxwell says, "People don't care how much you know until they know how much you care."

A Coat of Pain

In this case compassionate caring requires taking responsibility for understanding and communicating effectively the complex emotional landscapes involved with issues like abuse, addiction, and grief.

When discussing a new project we were working on, a man once asked me, "How did you recover from this when it happened in your life?" He expressed surprise and even a bit of anger when I confessed to him that I had not personally experienced the issue. "How can you write with any authenticity about something you haven't personally experienced?"

Though I'd never thought about it in these terms, I found myself drawing an analogy. "It's like each issue is a coat of pain hanging in a closet. When we're working on a project, I reach into the closet, take that coat of pain off of the hanger, and put it on."

I explained that I try to wear that coat as we interview people who have lived through the issue, as we talk with therapists and pastors who counsel them, and as we read the best material we can find on the topic. I try to see the issue from the inside out, and though I know this can only happen in a figurative sense, walk in the shoes of those who have lived it.

Once I think I have an understanding of what a particular experience feels like, then I use the canvas of a song to craft a lyric that speaks that truth. "When people who've lived through the issue listen and say, 'Yes! That's exactly how it feels!' then I know we've accomplished our goal."

If we want people to trust God, then I believe it is important that they know that God understands their pain and is with them in it. Songs that seek to reflect God have to ring true with lived experience. This approach has proved critical for songs on a number of our projects but never more so than on our resource for suicide grief, *Chaos of the Heart.*

The first two songs on the project pitch the tent I was talking about, digging deep into the pain and camping out there. The lyric of the title track takes direct aim at the confusion that all suicide grief survivors face:

> *I'm sorry and I'm sad*
> *and I'm hurting and I'm mad*
> *and I love you and I hate you*
> *and it makes me feel so bad*
> *The good is stained with evil*
> *They cannot be pulled apart*
> *Is there any healing from*
> *This chaos of the heart?*[1]

There is such misunderstanding around issues like these. And all too often, when silence and simply being present would be the best response, many Christians and many Christian songs respond with platitudes that are at best unhelpful and at worst hurtful. "She's in a better place." "God must've needed him in heaven." "God will never give you more than you can handle."

The ambiguity reflected in the lyric of "Chaos of the Heart" is matched by a sense of disquiet in the music. The unresolved nature of the words and music recognizes and affirms the ongoing conflict in the heart of the loved one left behind. One suicide survivor told me that it "captured the dichotomy of the emotions we feel."

I believe that when we are willing to speak this kind of truth in song we help the listeners to feel understood. We help them to feel as if they are not alone: "If there is a song about this that means I'm not the only one who has ever felt this way." In essence a song like this gives a person permission to feel what he or she is *already* feeling. This is no small gift in the wake of a traumatic event like suicide or abuse.

We can do the same thing for a friend by being willing to listen when they are in a difficult situation. Perhaps they may even have moments where they doubt their faith. At times like this we need to be willing to be uncomfortable. Instead of trying to prop up a person who is hurting with empty platitudes, we can simply give the gift of our presence, trusting that God understands.

A God who understands us, even when we don't understand ourselves, is a God worthy of our trust and worship. This is a God who walks with us in times of confusion and pain. Being understood in this way helps us to feel that we are not alone. This is a God in whom we can take refuge and comfort.

What Kind of God Would Let This Happen?

To take it a step further, I think that all too often in our songs—and in our prayers—we stop short of being honest with God. We want to please God so we hold back, not sharing our less-pleasant thoughts, ashamed of how we really feel. I have always found this puzzling. God knows our thoughts before we even express them so how does holding back what we are really feeling honor God? And yet, I do it all the same.

This is particularly true with anger. Many Christians have expressed to me the belief that "it's not OK to be angry with God."

Since every emotion we have is a gift from God, I figure that goes for anger too. God must have had a reason for giving us the emotion of anger. That's why I feel certain He can handle it, even when we direct our anger at Him.

God wants us to be in relationship with Him. We get angry with our spouses, our kids, our parents, our friends, and so on. If our relationship with God is to be authentic and genuine, there are going to be times when we may have to share that we are not happy with the way things are going.

To do so is not a lack of faith but quite the contrary. It demonstrates faith in a God who is big enough to handle whatever we are feeling, no matter how ugly or troubling it may be.

David, who God called "a man after my own heart" (Acts 13:22), certainly knew this. Look at Psalm 88:

> God knows our thoughts before we even express them.

> Why, LORD, do you reject me
> and hide your face from me?
> From my youth I have suffered and been close to death;
> I have borne your terrors and am in despair.
> Your wrath has swept over me;
> your terrors have destroyed me.
> All day long they surround me like a flood;
> they have completely engulfed me.
> You have taken from me friend and neighbor—
> darkness is my closest friend. (vv. 14–18)

It is with this perspective in mind that John Mandeville and I wrote the song "How Could You?" Originally the song was written as part of a full-length project on grief called *Dancing with Angels*, which John and I co-produced after the death of my wife's father.

When we finished the project, but before it was released, I shared the song with Christy, a devout Christian woman who worked in the same office with me. Her brother had recently been killed. She told me that the song "How Could You?" was the most meaningful song on the entire project. It gave vent to the anger she was feeling that God allowed her brother's life to be senselessly cut short.

Later I had to go back to her and tell her that the executive producer was not going to include "How Could You?" on the project. The reason that he gave was that he felt it was not OK to question God. I strenuously disagreed, but since he was paying for the record he had the final say.

Fast-forward eight years to when I was thinking of doing a full-length project on suicide grief. Tony Wood and I had written the song "Chaos of the Heart," but I had nothing else for the project. Shortly thereafter, the religion editor of the *The Tennessean* newspaper contacted me about doing an interview regarding Music for the Soul. I expected the story would be on an interior page of the religion section. A few days after we did the interview, the editor sent a photographer around to our office to take some pictures for the story. Imagine my surprise when, one Monday morning, the story appeared on the *front* page of *The Tennessean* above the fold, with a color photograph!

> He felt it was not OK to question God.

I soon heard from Sue Foster, a Christian counselor living in the San Diego, California, area. Sue, who had lost her daughter Shannon to a suicide death, was in the process of co-authoring the excellent book *Finding Your Way after the Suicide of Someone You Love*.[2] She had learned of Music for the Soul from a colleague in South Dakota who saw the online *Tennessean* article, in which I mentioned having just written "Chaos of the Heart." I was already planning to be in Los Angeles the following week so Sue agreed to drive up to LA so we could meet face-to-face. I never cease to be amazed at the ways God finds to connect our ministry to the person we need at just the right time!

Sue wound up being an invaluable consultant to the *Chaos of the Heart* resource and an important member of the Music for the Soul team. When I played "How Could You?" for Sue and asked if she thought it should be on *Chaos*, her response was swift and definitive. "Absolutely!"

The lyric reads in part:

> *What kind of God would let this happen?*
> *How could You be so unfair?*
> *You're the One whose love*
> *is supposed to be enough*
> *It feels like You don't even care*
>
> *I thought that I could trust You*
> *I thought I knew what You were like*
> *What did I do to deserve*
> *this cruel relentless hurt*
> *this bottomless void in my life*
>
> *How could You?*
> *Why didn't You step in and stop this?*
> *How could You bring me so much pain?*
> *In my deepest hour of need why did You abandon me?*
> *With nothing but Your silence to embrace*
> *How could You?*

God responds:

> *I'm the Lord your God who loves you*
> *Your rage is safe with Me*
> *I will never leave you*
> *I'll meet you where you'll meet Me*
> *Tell Me everything you're feeling*
> *You can't make Me turn away*
> *Let Me have your anger*
> *There's all kinds of ways to pray*
> *Talk to Me*[3]

Because I thought highly of the man who'd decided against including "How Could You?" on the *Dancing with Angels* project, I wondered if there might be some level of negative backlash from Christians disapproving of a song that expressed anger with God. None ever came. Instead we received a wave of responses from Christian survivors of suicide grief expressing their gratitude.

Then something remarkable happened that confirmed for me once and for all the importance of songs speaking with uncensored truth about God and life's deepest valleys.

One day there was a knock on the door of our Music for the Soul office in Nashville. It was a woman in her mid-forties. "May I come in?"

Sue Foster was with me at the time. We invited the lady in and offered her a seat on the couch, but she wasn't seated for long. She had to pace as she told her story.

"I'm a single mom. My seventeen-year-old son killed himself three months ago. He was my only child. He was my whole family." As she shared this devastating news, her voice was calm. Her sadness was palpable, and Sue and I felt helpless as we looked on.

The woman continued. "I was so angry at God that I couldn't pray. I just said, 'I'm done with You,' and I stopped speaking to Him altogether. I lost my faith. Then somebody gave me a copy of *Chaos of the Heart*, and I heard 'How Could You?' Before I knew it, I started screaming and raging at God, and I couldn't stop."

She said, "You gave me prayer language. All I'm doing is yelling at God, but at least we're talking again. Thank you."

After she left Sue and I sat in stunned silence, moved by what had just occurred. Her grief overwhelmed me. Her coming to see us overwhelmed me as well. I felt her coming had been a sacred gift.

I will never forget that day. The visit impacted me deeply and confirmed for me the vital importance of being willing to write about the hard truths. I feel as if God has shown me that people need to hear their stories told and their feelings shared, even if they are dark and painful to hear. As a follower of Christ and a song-writer, I feel the responsibility that comes with that knowledge.

How Do You Write a Song about That?

People will often ask, "How do write songs about _____ ? (fill in the blank). Because of this question I have actually taught a class called "How Do You Write a Song about That?"

My response is always the same. It doesn't matter whether the topic is suicide grief or pornography addiction or eating disorders. The songs are not about the issue.

The songs are about the feelings of the *people*. The songs are about the stories that make up human life in this fallen and broken world. Ultimately the songs are about the reconciling and redeeming love of God and the compassion and hope of Christ.

Most of all the songs are a conversation. They are an opportunity for listeners to hear a story that speaks their truth. As people identify with the truth in the song, they are invited to begin the process of their own healing.

I believe God is in the healing business, desiring for us to have the fullest expression of life, constantly inviting us to health and wholeness.

That's always a conversation worth having.

Songs from Chaos of the Heart *can be streamed at www.musicforthesoul.org/resources/chaos-of-the-heart.*

SOMEBODY'S DAUGHTER

"My heart…has often been solaced
and refreshed by music when sick and weary."
MARTIN LUTHER

Late one night several years ago my telephone rang. It was my friend John. He was at the point of total desperation. "I need to tell someone my secret, or I'm going to lose everything. I'm taking a chance that you're a safe place," he said. It was then John revealed to me that he was struggling deeply with pornography.

From the outside John had seemed to be the guy who had the world by the tail. A handsome, talented Christian songwriter, writing hits for groups like Avalon, 4Him, and Point of Grace, John appeared the epitome of success. He had a gorgeous wife and two precious, beautiful daughters. He was smart and had a great sense of humor and lots of friends.

But while from all appearances everything looked great, he was living a lie, hiding his secret shame from family and friends alike, and slipping deeper and deeper into emotional isolation and hopelessness.

That night on the phone John asked me if I would go to a sex addict's meeting with him because he didn't want to go alone. The next evening we did just that. Then, the following week we got together and processed what we had experienced at the meeting, which resulted in us writing a song called "Somebody's Daughter."

As fathers ourselves, the song would serve as a reminder for us to treat other people's daughters the way we want our own daughters to be treated. It was our way of planting a flag and making a pledge that from that day forward we would look at every woman as someone who has a mother and a father—and a *heavenly* Father.

The lyric reads in part:

> *Heaven's own precious child*
> *A person full of worth and dignity*
> *When her beauty is defiled*
> *I demean us both*
> *and fail to see*
>
> *She's somebody's daughter*
> *Somebody's child*
> *Somebody's pride and joy*
> *Somebody loves her for who she is inside*
> *She has a mother and father*
> *She's somebody's daughter*
> *She has a heavenly father*
> *She's somebody's daughter*[1]

When I wrote that song I was just trying to help a dear friend. I had no idea that God would use this message to touch lives around the world.

However, it became clear fairly soon after writing "Somebody's Daughter" that John's problem was much more common than I had realized. In discreetly discussing the issue with friends in the Christian music industry, I found out within just a few weeks that I knew seven—*seven*—other men, either Christian recording artists or Christian songwriters, who were struggling with pornography. I thought, *Surely this can't be just a Christian music industry problem.*

So I started doing the research. It was like picking at some chipped, dry paint in the corner of a wall and then having the whole wall come off in your hands. What I found was frightening. Pornography use was pandemic not only in the culture but in the church. I talked with a Promise Keepers event leader who said more than half of the men attending their most recent gathering had admitted to viewing pornography within the last month. At about the same time I saw the results of a survey done by Focus on the Family where 40 percent of pastors had privately admitted to having a problem with pornography.

Since then, things have only gotten worse. Much worse.

Because men feel such shame over acting out with pornography, it is something they tend to hide and find incredibly difficult to talk about.* For this reason the approach of broaching the subject in a full-length CD became immensely important. This would be something that they could listen to privately. Hopefully it could be a lifeline for men who heard it, the first step toward recognizing their problem and getting help. I could also imagine men hearing these songs and thinking, *If there is a song about this, then I can't be the only one who is struggling with it!* Additionally, I felt it would give the loved ones and friends of those struggling with pornography a less confrontational way to begin a dialogue.

This feeling was confirmed when Pamela from Texas wrote to me. Her husband Grant† had been secretly fighting a pornography problem for years. Partners in ministry, married nineteen years with four children, his confession of pornography use had rocked their marriage. "I felt as if I didn't really know the man I had shared

---

* Now an ever-increasing number of women are struggling with pornography as well.
† Not their real names

my life with." Finally she told him, "I will leave you if you don't get help."

Grant at last got up the courage to go to a support group. That's where a new friend gave him a copy of the *Somebody's Daughter* CD. "He listened over and over as the songs helped relieve him of the burden of shame," Pamela said. "He couldn't believe there were other men that struggled at the deep level he had. Finally, he felt hopeful that if other men had gotten victory over lust, perhaps he could experience freedom as well."

> "The songs helped relieve him of the burden of shame."

So, how did a song I wrote for the purpose of helping one friend wind up being a song that has helped men and families I've never met, many in places I will never go?

As I talked with more and more men and their wives (or ex-wives), it wasn't the numbers that bothered me. It was the true stories of lives being ripped apart. I didn't want to get caught up in the mind-numbing numbers and forget that each number represented a story—a real life in danger of being destroyed.

I did almost a hundred radio interviews after the release of *Somebody's Daughter*. Every time I was on the radio to discuss the pornography issue, the first thing the host would ask me was, "Steve, what are the statistics?" I understood that they were trying to establish for their audiences that pornography was a problem, but that question always frustrated me. I think this is because by that point I had realized that pornography was affecting *everybody*. My frustration then, and now, was based on the fact that people still needed convincing.

I began to respond to the question by asking, "What chance do you think a child who starts kindergarten in the U.S. today has of graduating from high school without seeing pornography?" Of course it is a rhetorical question.

In this culture the answer is *no chance at all*.

Still later, when people protested that pornography was not a problem in their life, I began to use the analogy of a swimming pool. Our culture is the water in the pool. You may only swim in the shallow end. But if someone is continuously poisoning the water in the deep end of the pool, eventually that's going to affect you. In other words, just because you don't personally look at pornography doesn't make you immune from its corrosive effect on society. The more pornography is "normalized," the more pervasive and inescapable its impact becomes on things that each of us interact with every day—things like the Internet, the media, and the attitudes of our friends and neighbors.

Pornography is not God's will for our lives.

Of course, there *are* statistics. Lots of them. A quick search of the web will turn up some alarming numbers.[2]

But putting numbers aside for the moment, let me say this unequivocally. Pornography is not God's will for our lives, our marriages, our families, or our churches. Pornography *kills*. It kills love. It kills intimacy. It kills marriages. It kills families. I have personally known men who have become addicted, men who have gone bankrupt, men who have become impotent, men who have gotten divorced, men who have lost access to their children, and even men who have gone to prison—lives all destroyed because of pornography.

It was with all of this in mind that John Mandeville and I turned our attention to writing a collection of songs that would speak honestly about the issue of pornography—from being trapped in its grip, to realizing the need for help, to confessing the problem to others, to walking through the steps toward healing, and ultimately to finding freedom.

Is it Me?

John and I ultimately wrote seven songs. We felt that it was important that one of the songs speak directly from the spouse's point of view. So often a woman will feel that she must have done something to cause her husband to be unfaithful to her in this way. "If only I'd been pretty enough. If only I'd kept the weight off." These are just a few of the self-blaming comments I've heard over and over again from women. That is how John and I came to write the song "Is It Me?"

In Matthew 5:28 Jesus says "anyone who looks at a woman lustfully has already committed adultery with her in his heart." Based on this definition, pornography use *is* adultery.

Christian therapists have described to me the collision of conflicting emotions spouses feel when they discover their partner has betrayed them with pornography. This is because the very person they would normally lean on for help is the source of the problem.

We wanted to create a song that would help men understand this and understand the reality of the pain they had caused their spouse. At the same time we were hoping to assure women that the contradictory feelings they were experiencing were normal.

John's wife Shelli is an incredible singer in her own right. I asked her if she would be willing to come into the studio and record "Is It Me?" First Shelli sang:

> *I can't breathe*
> *This can't be happening to me*
> *Was everything we had just a lie?*
> *I believed while you deceived me*
> *Faithful while my love was being violated*
> *Nothing is the same*
> *Nothing to hold on to*
> *Where's the man I knew a day ago?*[3]

Then I asked her to do something extremely difficult.

"Just for a moment I want you to remember how you felt when you first found out about the pornography use and I want you to channel all that rage into the microphone." Courageously, she agreed. Then we prayed together before she went into the vocal booth. The fury she unleashed when we went into record mode had the guys in the studio looking for the exits!

Having captured that anger on the recording, I then said, "OK, I want you to do it again, but this time, I want you to say all the things into the microphone that you *wish* you could have said to your husband at that moment." Shelli then proceeded to break our hearts, expressing her desires in a tender voice.

When she was done, we put the two recordings together. The final result reflects the diametrically opposed feelings a woman experiences when she discovers her husband has betrayed her with pornography.

> *HOW COULD YOU DO THIS TO ME?!?!*
> *i can tell you're sorry*
> *DON'T TOUCH ME!!!*
> *i need you to hold me.*
> *IT'S OVER BETWEEN US!*
> *i know this isn't like you*
> *I HATE YOU!!!*
> *i hate that i need you*

It may sound strange, but I really felt the Holy Spirit's presence empowering Shelli to capture what was needed to comfort the women who would listen.

Later, after the song was released, a woman called me to say that she felt like she was going insane until she heard this song. "It spoke my feelings exactly. I just sobbed and sobbed. I felt so relieved that what I was feeling was normal."

Another woman wrote saying that she couldn't "believe someone put into words what I was feeling." She said she had sat in her car and played the song for other women who had just discovered their husbands were involved with pornography. "It is the song I come to."

In addition to the new songs John and I wrote, we also pulled in three existing songs. One of those was a song I had co-written with Scott Krippayne and Kent Hooper a few years earlier for one of Scott's solo projects.

> We prayed together before she went into the vocal booth.

Scott had given me a piece of music that he and Kent had written and asked me to write some words for it. The music was rather unsettling in its tone, and I hadn't been sure exactly what the lyric should say.

Then one night after my wife went to bed, I was channel surfing. As I was flipping channels, something—shall we say "inappropriate"—came on the screen. I lingered for a moment. Not long. Maybe ten seconds. But it was long enough to feel the shame of having seen something that I should not have seen. Why hadn't I changed the channel right away? Almost immediately I became very angry with myself for my act of weakness. How could I have allowed myself to dishonor God and my wife in this way? I went downstairs to my office and grabbed a blank pad. In ten minutes the lyric was done:

> *No one's watching*
> *Now I'll find out if You're real to me*
> *Will I love You*
> *or give into something less in me?*
> *How long will my mistakes keep rehearsing?*
> *Jesus*
> *I've taken liberties with Your mercy*

All of me
I need to surrender all my favorite sins
Let You in to places I have never let You in
I come clean
Lord, take all of me
You know my hand
All the cards I never show the world
No more bluffing
I cast down these artificial pearls[4]

Even though it was late, I called Scott as soon as I had completed the lyric. "This might not have been what you were looking for," I told him. But after reading to him what I had written, he courageously agreed to record it. He didn't change a word.

The final piece to the puzzle was a song John had written by himself. It was called "Free." At that time he said, "It's not a statement of where I am. It is a statement of where I'm going."

A Voice Restored

With the songs in place, production of *Somebody's Daughter* began. God's hand was miraculously present on multiple occasions in the production of the CD. The last day before we were to send the final recording to be mastered we still didn't have a testimony in place to introduce the title track.

I called my friend Larry Watkins, a Christian counselor who works with men and couples around the issue of sex addiction. As I mentioned earlier, Larry introduced me to one of my favorite sayings: "Jesus knows *everybody!*" I thought perhaps someone he had counseled in the past might be willing to come to the studio and give a testimony.

Sure enough he knew someone he thought would be willing to speak for the recording. The following day when the man arrived we exchanged introductions, and then I got him situated in the vocal booth on a folding chair in front of a microphone. He asked me, "What should I say?"

I said, "I don't want to be directive. Just say whatever you'd like to say in your own words." He knew the project was about overcoming a struggle with pornography, but that was all Larry had told him. I didn't tell him the title of the project.

We began recording, and a chill ran up and down my spine as almost the first words out of his mouth were, "You look at your own daughter or your friends' daughters, and you think 'Wow,' that could be the person you were looking at or lusting over on the computer. Or your friends could be doing the same thing to your daughter. When you really start thinking about it, that's disgusting."

He ended his statement with an uncomfortable gallows laugh. I could not believe it. If I had scripted his words, I could not have come up with a better introduction to the title track, "Somebody's Daughter."

When it came time to choose a singer for the title song, to me there was only one option. Clay Crosse had been a chart-topping singer with a soaring voice in the mid to late nineties in contemporary Christian music. Unbeknownst to his wife, his record label, and his fans, Clay was secretly struggling with a pornography problem. In the late nineties, Clay began to have vocal problems, and the soaring tenor voice with the wonderful range that had made him so popular became unreliable.

Clay believes that God took his voice away to get his attention. It worked. Clay confessed his struggles to his wife, Renee, putting concern for his marriage and family before his career.* In the aftermath of confessing his struggles with pornography, Clay and Renee were able to work together to get him the help he needed and to

---

* Renee Crosse shares part of her testimony on the *Somebody's Daughter* CD.

heal their marriage. They now have a wonderful ministry together called Holy Homes.[5] As of this writing, Clay is also the worship leader of a church in Bentonville, Arkansas.

At the time we were getting ready to record the vocal track for "Somebody's Daughter," I was concerned that Clay might not be able to bring his former power as a singer to the song. But with his own history and being a father of daughters himself, I knew that he understood the heart of this song in a deeply personal way. For that reason I invited him to sing it.

When he stepped into the vocal booth that day, I soon knew that my concerns were unfounded. He performed the song with passion and conviction and hit all the high notes effortlessly. God had restored Clay's voice.

Something Very Brave

Once the *Somebody's Daughter* CD was released, stories poured in about how the songs were turning lives around—helping to set men free and saving and transforming marriages.

One of these stories came from a man named John Cozart. He told me that *Somebody's Daughter* played a pivotal role in his healing. "I listened to that CD over and over," he said. "Oh how it spoke to me. That is when I decided 'enough is enough.' Make no mistake about it; God orchestrated the placement of the *Somebody's Daughter* CD into my hands."

And God orchestrated it in quite an unusual way. John's friend Dave and his wife Carol were driving on a country road through a remote area of South Carolina and were having no luck at all finding a radio station to listen to. Then finally, through crackle and static, they found a Christian station. The station was talking about *Somebody's Daughter* and played the song.

It made an impression upon Dave, who had suspected pornography might be an issue for his friend. So when he got home to Florida, Dave went online and ordered a copy of the *Somebody's Daughter* CD, which he later shared with John.

Cozart went on to start his own ministry to help men who had a problem with pornography. Later, he arranged for us to do a live presentation of the entire *Somebody's Daughter* CD at his home church in the Orlando, Florida, area.

John Mandeville and I were sitting in the living room of the Cozart home a few days before the presentation when a local businessman and his wife stopped by. The story this man told absolutely floored us.

> Songs were turning lives around.

"My wife and I had not had sex in twenty years," the man said. "She'd had a disabling surgery that had left her in quite a bit of pain so I turned to pornography to satisfy my sexual desires. Once she got better, we just sort of agreed not to talk about it, or so I thought.

"We went on that way for two decades until a friend of mine recognized the symptoms and gave me a copy of the *Somebody's Daughter* CD. I listened to the songs and they convicted me."

Then this man did something very brave.

"I went to my wife and I said I want you to listen to this with me. We listened together. And then we cried and then we fought and then we cried and then we fought and then we fought and then we cried. And then we were intimate for the first time in twenty years. You gave me back my wife."

A few nights later as John Mandeville sang "Free," I watched as men and women of every age streamed down to the front of the church to ask for prayer and for help with their problem with pornography, the song inviting them to move beyond their shame to a place of hope and restoration.

John Cozart has since been responsible for thousands of people being reached by *Somebody's Daughter*—and brought his wisdom and skill to the ministry of Music for the Soul as a board member.

More importantly, he has become a close personal friend, yet another example of how God has used a ministry I started in hopes of blessing others to richly bless me. We can't out-give God!

A String of "Coincidences"

No sooner had the *Somebody's Daughter* CD come out when people started asking me, "Where is the DVD?"

As Corey Niemchick of Storytelling Pictures and I brainstormed about what such a project should look like, it quickly became evident that this would be by far the most expensive undertaking yet for Music for the Soul. I was still wondering how we were going to go about finding the budget when it came time for our ministry to have a booth at the biannual American Association of Christian Counselors conference.

During the conference a woman named Judi Reid came up to our booth, pausing to peruse our catalog of resources. "I'll take one of each," she said. This was on a Thursday.

The following Monday she called our office. She'd spent the weekend listening to our material and was impressed. "What are you working on now?" she wanted to know.

I told her that we were planning to do a DVD based on the *Somebody's Daughter* CD.

"When is the next filming date?" she asked.

"We don't have anything scheduled yet," I replied. "We would need around $20,000 before we could even think about putting a shoot together."

"Oh. I'll send that today," Judi said.

Startled, I responded, "Ma'am?" I wasn't sure I had heard her correctly.

"I'll send that today," she repeated.

When her gift was matched two days later, she said, "That was too easy. I'll send another ten."

And that's how our *Somebody's Daughter* production budget went from $0 to $50,000 in forty-eight hours. One week Judi and I didn't know each other existed. A week later we were working together on a project that has touched millions of hurting lives with the love and compassion of Christ.

Jesus knows everybody!!!

When production began on the *Somebody's Daughter* DVD,[6] it was to include about forty minutes of powerful personal testimony, some vignettes telling the story of a young family, and three song videos.

The song "Never Shake His Hand," written by Rick Altizer, is a cautionary tale about what can happen when we invite evil into our lives. In the context of *Somebody's Daughter*, it perfectly illustrates the insidiousness of pornography and the way it masquerades as harmless "entertainment" when it is, in fact, toxic poison.

To underscore this message, Storytelling Pictures came up with a variety of creative and compelling visual images for the music video. How creative? Let's just say when I started Music for the Soul I never imagined any scenario involving a train, a bowl of rotting fruit, and a burning house. The *Never Shake His Hand* music video has all of these and much more.

When scoping out the property that was to be burned for the shoot, the Storytelling team found only one thing in the otherwise empty house. And I'll bet you can already guess what it was. A stash of pornography was in the bedroom closet. They left it there, and when the house catches on fire in the video, the pornography goes up in flames with it.

As we neared the end of production on the *Somebody's Daughter* DVD, something was troubling me. God impressed upon me that we weren't done. I couldn't shake this feeling that something was missing. Then suddenly it landed on me. There was nothing on the DVD specifically for youth, for those in their teens and early twenties.

I didn't know what we were going to do. The budget was gone. And even if we had had a budget, we had no song. But little did I know God had already put in motion events that would lead to a *fourth* song video for the project.

As it happened that weekend, I was participating in a Write About Jesus workshop in Nashville. This was the first time the workshop had ever taken place outside of the St. Louis, Missouri, area.

One of the standard elements of every Write About Jesus Conference is a song critique. Registrants sign up to have their songs listened to and judged by a duo of professional writers. In this case there were seven different sign-up sheets, seven different opportunities for writers to have their songs critiqued.

My partner in the critique session was a writer named Chad Cates. Chad had come to me while we were working on the original *Somebody's Daughter* CD and asked if he could write for the project, which he did, eventually contributing to the song "Every Man's Battle." When Chad and I were seated and ready to begin, we asked for a volunteer to have his or her song played first. A handsome young man in a brown cloth cap slid his CD across the table and said, "I guess I'll go first."

It's important to mention here that many of the songs we listen to in critique sessions at Write About Jesus, especially from beginning writers, can sometimes be a little rough. In fact, Topher immediately began apologizing for his performance of the song before we even started playing it.

The lyric sheet said "Losing Ground," Words & Music by Topher Teague. No sooner had the song began than Chad and I exchanged a glance. The song was very good. The vocal and guitar performance were also excellent. But even more amazing than all of that was the topic of the song: pornography.

As each line of the song unfolded, I got more and more excited. This was the missing piece we needed to complete the *Somebody's Daughter* DVD! After class I asked Topher if he would be interested

in Music for the Soul producing a video of his song. He enthusias-
tically replied yes. I also asked him to send to me an MP3 copy of
the song by e-mail.

OK, so now I had the song we needed. Not only that, I had
the singer. Topher was very talented and would be able to perform
for the recording as well as provide the band. But this was still only
half of the solution. Where were we going to get the money to
shoot another music video?

On the following Monday I called Corey Niemchick at
Storytelling Pictures. "We've got a problem," I said. "There's nothing on this DVD that speaks specifically to young people. We need
something to equip youth pastors."

Then I told him about the song that God had presented to me
at Write About Jesus. "Send me the MP3," Corey said.

The very next day Corey called. He and his business partner
John had listened to the song and wanted to make me an offer. "We
believe in this project, and we want it to be right. If you'll cover
the flight for us to come down to Nashville, we will shoot a music
video for this song free of charge."

I readily agreed. As it turns out, they decided to make the trip
on their motorcycles so I didn't even have to buy plane tickets!

Later on, when Topher and I were working on the arrangement
of the song at the Music for the Soul office, he shared with me that
he hadn't planned on going to Write About Jesus. His grandmother
in Murfreesboro, Tennessee, had seen an ad for the conference in
the paper, signed him up, paid for it, and said, "You need to go to
this."

That got me to thinking of the string of "coincidences" that
needed to come together for the song "Losing Ground" to find its
way on to the *Somebody's Daughter* DVD:

1. Write About Jesus had to be in Nashville for the first and
    only time in its fifteen-year history.

2. Topher's grandmother had to see the ad in the Murfreesboro newspaper.

3. Topher had to accept his grandmother's invitation to attend the conference.

4. Once there, he had to sign up for the critique session with Chad and me. If he had chosen to attend any one of the other six sessions, I would have never heard the song.

5. That's not all. Of the dozens of songs he had written, Topher had to decide to enter "Losing Ground" for a critique. (Pretty bold, considering he did so in a room full of strangers, most of whom were female. Certainly a very vulnerable choice!)

6. Then, once I determined that we should include the song, Corey and John had to decide to record a video for which we had absolutely *zero* budget available.

7. Finally, all of this had to happen precisely within the narrow time frame we had in order to fit into our production schedule.

I love it when God shows off!

I love it when God shows off!

The Song in Every Human Heart

Here is the truth. Instant private access to the Internet and cable television, the growth of social media, and the proliferation of cell phones, laptop computers, and iPads has exponentially increased the risk for exposure and access to pornography, especially for young people.

There are now many reliable studies showing that prolonged exposure to pornography rewires the neural pathways in the brain and compromises a person's capacity to experience healthy intimacy in a relationship.[7] Again, this makes the easy access of pornography especially troubling for young people who are absorbing this material *before* having had the opportunity to experience the beauty and wonder of a close relationship. This can't be the kind of corrosive environment in which we want our children and grandchildren to grow up.

Fortunately, several fine ministries and organizations are doing wonderful work in this area, specifically to educate people about the dangers of pornography and to provide help.[8]

It is my prayer that, when it comes to pornography, God will help our society work toward the day when no man or woman will have to live in shame, no marriage will have to end in heartbreak, and no child will have to lose his or her family.

It is my prayer that, when it comes to pornography, "Free" will become the song in every human heart.

Songs from Somebody's Daughter *may be streamed at www.musicforthesoul.org/resources/ somebodys-daughter.*

12

BINDER OF THE BROKEN

"Music has the power to move a person between different realities:
from a broken body into a soaring spirit;
from a broken heart into the connection of shared love;
from death into the movement and memory of life."
DR. DEFORIA LANE

After the devastating Gulf Coast hurricanes of 2005 hit, I was immediately contacted by people asking, "Is Music for the Soul going to do something for the hurricane victims?" This presented two big challenges.

First, whatever response we made would need to be swift. Thanksgiving was less than two months away. I felt that anything we did would need to be available in time for the holidays because Thanksgiving was going to be tough in New Orleans and the coastal areas of Mississippi.

Second, we had no money on hand for a new recording.

Complicating matters, a disproportionate amount of the damage had happened in the lower Ninth Ward, predominately an African-American community. The federal government's response was experienced as painfully slow and insufficient. The result was that within just the first few days in the aftermath of the storm racial tension became a big part of the story. As a white man—and an outsider—I felt I might not have an appropriate understanding of the issues involved. I didn't want to do anything that would offend the very people we intended to help.

The money issue was handled in a matter of a few days when a generous group of Christian businessmen in Florida, desiring to remain anonymous no less, donated the entire budget for the record. The racial challenge was answered in a variety of ways over the course of the next few weeks. In fact, it had already begun to be answered a few weeks before the hurricanes, though I didn't realize it at the time.

One morning I was at my desk when an e-mail came in from my friend Clarence Church, an African-American worship leader and songwriter who was living in Colorado at the time. There was a song attached.

I clicked play and went about looking over some paperwork. Within seconds, I involuntarily pushed back from the desk and closed my eyes, drinking in the music. The song, "Binder of the Broken," beautifully conveyed God's healing and redemptive nature. I knew we would have to do something special with it because it captured the spirit of Music for the Soul so beautifully.

A Song Finds Me

A few weeks later, as I considered what kind of songs we needed for the hurricane response record, it suddenly occurred to me. "Binder of the Broken," with its bittersweet and tender tone, could serve to offer comfort not only for the physical and emotional wounds caused by the hurricanes. It could also address the need for healing of the chasm between the races, the need for which had been laid bare by the contentious rhetoric in the wake of the storms. I thought that perhaps having the song performed as a duet between a man and a woman, one black and one white, would add a layer of meaning to the song that might reinforce the message of healing and reconciliation.

During a phone call, Clarence told me he had always been a Lisa Bevill fan. It just so happened that I knew Lisa. I told Clarence that if he could come to Nashville I would invite Lisa to sing a duet with him on "Binder." He told me that he would love to but that money was tight. Someone in the church office overheard his end of our conversation and offered to buy a plane ticket for Clarence on the spot! A few short weeks later we had captured one of the most stirring recordings in the Music for the Soul catalog.

Once "Binder of the Broken" was in place, I felt like we had taken a good step toward addressing the racial aspect dimension of the crisis in New Orleans. But I was still an outsider.

With that in mind I made two separate phone calls, one each to the two people I knew who had roots in New Orleans.

From time to time throughout the years, I have taught at seminars given for aspiring Christian singers and artists. As mentioned in the previous chapter, often a part of these events is the option to have a song critiqued by a music business professional.

At a Gospel Music Association event in Nashville, I had listened to the song of a young youth pastor from New Orleans named James Tealy. His song was exceptionally fresh in both its lyrical and musical approach so I asked him to stay after class, and we wound up having lunch together.

No sooner had we sat down than he pulled a CD out of his coat pocket and said, "I'm glad you liked my song, but I've got a girl here you really need to listen to."

I was intrigued. It's not every day that somebody uses his chance to make some headway in his own musical career and immediately begins to promote somebody else. The girl, Sara Beth Geoghegan* was one of the kids from his youth group in New Orleans.

---

* Pronounced Go-hay-gan

I really did intend to listen right away, but good intentions notwithstanding, I have to admit I tossed the CD into my car. It landed on the floor on the passenger side where it passed several weeks undisturbed. Then one day, while tooling down 16th Street on Music Row, I picked it up. I literally remember thinking, *Why do I have* this? I pulled the disk out of the sleeve and popped it in my car CD player. I was stunned. Her work was exceptional.

With sensitive and evocative lyrics, haunting bittersweet melodies, rich and complex harmonies, a lovely voice, and a profound sense of style, this young lady's work immediately captivated me. The first time Sara Beth came to our house and played a song for me on my piano I called out to my wife, "Honey, come quick!!! Joni Mitchell is in the house!"

Sara Beth—and, I am happy to say, also James—went on to sign staff songwriting deals and eventually record solo albums.[1]

For *After the Storm*, I called Sara Beth, a New Orleans native, and asked if she would write and record something for the album. I felt very strongly that the album should have a song that would give people permission to remember their city as it *had* been— a sort of memory postcard. The assignment I gave her was specific and daunting.

The song she wrote, "Trust Jesus,"* is full of iconic imagery of New Orleans and is by any measure a masterpiece. The recording, complimented by an elegantly understated Phillip Keveren string arrangement, achieved the desired effect to perfection.

I called James Tealy as well, and he delivered a song ironically called "Permanent." The lyric contrasts the temporal nature of possessions with the eternal love of Christ.

---

* Also known as "Sweeter"

Something wind and water
Cannot wash away²

Finally, we figured no recording meant to bless the people of New Orleans would be complete without "When the Saints Go Marching In." But I wanted to do something different with it, something more prayerful.

I called a wonderful studio singer I know named Debi Selby to put together a trio of female singers for an a cappella rendition. On the day of the session, Debi brought Delores Cox and Melinda Doolittle to the studio. Together they created a very moving, soulful rendition of the old spiritual.

There was a brief solo moment in the arrangement, and the ladies decided amongst themselves that Melinda should sing it. Little did we know, Melinda would soon attract national attention on *American Idol*.

Something's Missing

While songs began to come together quickly for the project, it was Sue in our office who first noticed that a crucial piece was missing.

"Where is the song that says that this is awful!?!" she exclaimed.

She was completely right of course. A distinguishing feature of Music for the Soul recordings from the beginning has been our willingness to tackle hard truths without any sugar coating—to give people permission to feel anger, pain, and confusion or any other difficult emotion. Rather than resolving these emotions by the end of the song, our approach is to have at least one song on every record that states the pain and ends without resolution. This way the feelings of the listener are acknowledged right where they are. The listener feels validated and understood.

I began to search my thoughts for an idea that might effectively convey the sense of loss and displacement I had heard expressed by many of the evacuees who had spoken with us. The idea of "Where Is the Ground?" came to me, perhaps as a result of seeing days of news coverage of endless piles of debris and whole city blocks submerged.

Sometimes an idea comes, and the song rolls out right behind it, as happened with "More Beautiful" and "Whole in the Sight of God." But after a whole week, all I had was the title for "Where Is the Ground?"

The following weekend my wife and I were staying at a bed and breakfast in Monterey, Tennessee, attending the wedding of a friend. While lying in bed on Friday night, waiting for sleep, the lines of the first verse started to come into my head.

The following morning at sunrise I went outside to see if anymore of the lyric would come. We'd arrived the previous night, and I was not prepared for the view that greeted me. The bed and breakfast was perched on a cliff overlooking a small canyon with a view out to the east, the Cumberland Plateau rising in the distance.

I sat down on the rocks, marveling at the beauty of the scene before me, and the words began to flow . . . and right behind them came the melody. The whole song came in forty-five minutes.

Why a setting of such serenity and natural beauty unlocked words of pain and devastation I do not know. I must confess that even after writing songs for more than thirty years I still don't have any magic formula for getting started. Sometimes I think an idea just needs time to swim around in the subconscious before it is ready to be born.

When I got back to Nashville, I played the song through on the piano and still felt good about it. However, I was concerned about whether the music would resonate for those from New Orleans and for African-American listeners in particular. With that in mind I contacted an old friend of mine named Tim Lauer. I knew

Tim played several instruments and was good on the squeezebox,*
which I thought was the best place to begin to try and give the song
some New Orleans flavor.

After hearing the song, Tim was pumped, so much so that he
actually talked me out of hiring him!

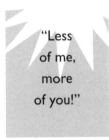

"Less of me, more of you!"

"It's a good song, but I'm not the right guy
for it. Let me tell you the vision I see for it. We're
in an African-American church somewhere down
in Mississippi or Louisiana. There's a wall missing or maybe the roof's been blown off, but the
people are still there to worship."

Before I even had a chance to agree, he continued excitedly, "You need to call Mark Harris!"

Mark Harris is a tremendously talented, well-established black
gospel musician who played with the likes of BeBe Winans and
Michael McDonald before starting his own record label.

"I don't know Mark," I said.

"He goes to my church," said Tim, looking up the number.

Seeing it all come together, I asked Tim what I should do next.

"Play the song for Mark then ask *him* who should sing it," he
suggested.

So I did. A few days later Mark and I met for a cup of coffee,
and I played the song for him. He immediately recommended that
I ask Keith Floyd to sing the vocal. Ten days later we recorded the
piano, organ, and lead vocal at Dark Horse Studios in Franklin,
Tennessee.

Mark came in knowing my work tape a little too well. During
the first few takes, I felt like something wasn't working, and then
I realized he was trying to replicate what he had heard me play on
the demo. Through the studio glass, I found myself shouting to
Mark, "Less of me, more of you!" In no time he was playing soulful

---

* Accordion

riffs that my fingers could only dream of. Then it was Keith's turn to shine. His friend Derek Armstrong had come along to the session, and it was a good thing, too, because he kept pushing Keith to new heights I didn't even know he was capable of. I might have settled for less than his best.

Once all of the performances were captured, my co-producer Kent Hooper took the recording back to the House of Big to mix. He called me a day or two later and said, "You know what this needs now is some church ambience."

A few minutes later he was downloading a recording of background noise from a Mt. Zion Baptist Church somewhere in Georgia. But once that was added—complete with people talking, creaking pews, and even a few coughs—Kent called back again with another idea.

"You know what this needs now, don't you?" he asked rhetorically.

"A real preacher!"

For some reason, now becoming clear, I had left a section of twenty seconds of instrumental music between the end of the bridge and the beginning of the last chorus.

I called my wife about Kent's new idea, and she immediately suggested, "Why don't you call Dr. Crowder?"

I had heard Rev. William Crowder preach on two occasions previously. I agreed with my wife that he would be perfect.

A few evenings later we were in the studio with a black gospel choir working on the background vocals for "City of Hope" and "Binder of the Broken" when it occurred to me that if we were going to have a black preacher on the recording, then we were going to need the call and response of a African-American congregation church meeting! At the end of the session, I asked the singers to imagine they were in a service and were talking back to the preacher. Two minutes later we had a wonderful variety of enthusiastic "responses."

The following morning Dr. Crowder came into the studio. In the song, the question "Where is God?" is posed by the lyric at the end of the bridge. Dr. Crowder delivered a thundering affirmation of the presence of God in the midst of tragedy. With the miraculous technology we have for recording nowadays, we were able to place the replies of the "congregation" wherever we needed them to achieve the sense of a live worship service.

Dr. Crowder would not be the only one to speak meaningful words of hope and wisdom on the project. As we prayed for this project to come together in time for Thanksgiving, it was amazing how the right spoken-word pieces showed up. For example, one morning I went to the post office box where I found a CD from a lady who attended a church in *Denver, Colorado*—not famous for its hurricanes. On that disc was a sermon piece with a segment that wound up being the perfect introduction for one of the New Orleans songs.

A Gift of Reconciliation

In the weeks following Hurricane Katrina, thousands of displaced residents from New Orleans were scattered across the southeast. One morning Sue Foster and I went to Centennial Park in Nashville where a large group of storm refugees were gathered. We wanted to see if we could find some people who would be willing to tell their stories on the recording.

That's where we met Hank and Lyndia. The Handys had a harrowing story of survival that culminated in Hank asking to receive Christ as his Lord and Savior. He had been baptized just a few days after the storm.

Though we soon lost track of Hank and Lyndia—after all they had no cell phone and literally only the clothes on their backs!—we were miraculously reconnected with them through one of the many shelters that had been set up around town. We invited them to come into the studio a few days later so Hank could tell his story.

When they arrived I interviewed Hank for several minutes. He was a little microphone shy, but his description of the flood is what we ultimately used to open the CD. When he was done I turned to Lyndia.

"Since you're here, would you like to say anything?"

She replied, "Being Creole, there was no bathroom for me. My black side says, 'You made me a slave.' My white side says, 'I hurt you.' . . . There is no racism in God. . . . Where is your compassion? Where is your forgiveness?" she pleaded. Chills ran up and down my spine.

> It is Jesus who is the Binder of the broken.

The testimony that poured out of Lyndia Handy captured the spirit of the message we wanted to share better than anything I could have ever written—the message that it is Jesus who is the Binder of the broken.

The finished result of *After the Storm* is something I could never have imagined. When people ask me if I produce the Music for the Soul recordings, I always smile. Only God can orchestrate the events that could make a piece like *After the Storm* possible. Through God's grace and the shared talents of some very gifted new friends, I believe we achieved the authenticity I was hoping and praying for.

Therapists tell me now that the songs created in the wake of that disaster are helpful for those dealing with issues of loss and depression around a whole range of issues. One Christian counselor told me, "I used 'Where Is the Ground?' to help a man who was going through an unwanted divorce."

It made sense. When you hear a song about a storm, it's the storms in *your* life that it speaks to.

Fifty-eight days after Katrina struck the Gulf Coast, we gave away 15,000 copies of *After the Storm* to communities that had been impacted by the storms. Pastor Louis Husser of Crossgate Baptist Church in Robert, Louisiana, told me, "Thank you. After food, the thing my people need the most is music." Pastor David Crosby of First Baptist Church in New Orleans said, "The songs and testimonies speak to our hearts and help us deal with the daily experience of seeing the devastation. They give us hope, and we need that more than anything."

Karen in Mandeville, Louisiana, wrote, "Your music somehow reminds me that it is safe for me to come out; that someone wants to carry it for me and will be with me for the long haul. Thanks for awakening my heart again to the Lord's comfort and love. It has renewed my faith and hope and is helping me to grieve the many losses that have come our way."

We also received a startling response from an emergency medical technician who had served in the wake of the disaster. She had seen so much devastation that she was considering suicide: "Tonight I felt like ending my life and as a Christian I don't understand that. But I was touched by your music. I truly, truly needed you guys and you were there. Thank you so very much."

Like these and many others who reached out to us, I too am grateful. I'm grateful for the gifts God gives us to help us get through, and carry on after, the storms in our lives. Gifts like each other. Gifts like music. And I'm so grateful for the privilege of being able, through the songs, to walk with people experiencing heartache and despair, bringing them the real hope of Jesus Christ.

Songs from After the Storm *may be streamed at www.musicforthesoul.org/resources/ after-the-storm.*

13

TELL ME WHAT YOU SEE

"Music is one of the ways we can achieve
a kind of shorthand to understand each other."
YO-YO MA

I began working at A&M Records in the late seventies. My job was in the merchandising department. We created and distributed items to help promote albums and tours—things such as posters, T-Shirts, coffee mugs, and so on. During my time at A&M, there began to be a lot of talk about music videos. In only a few years, music videos became mainstream, and by 1985 Mark Knopfler of Dire Straits was singing, "I want my MTV."

At first I was excited about music videos. I imagined, quite erroneously as it turned out, that music videos would capture live performances of the songs by the artists in concert or perhaps the recording of a song in the studio.

Then I remember hearing Joe Jackson, an artist with A&M at the time, talking about the unfair advantage music videos were going to provide for the more beautiful people among the recording artists. This reminded me of the argument that Abraham Lincoln would have never been elected president of the United States in the age of television. Jackson's observation was the first hint to me that perhaps music videos weren't actually going to be about the music.

Of course, here we are thirty years or so later, and now every music single put out by the industry has its own mini-movie. Now we *see* the music. Sometimes the story these videos tell will have something to do with the lyric, if only marginally. Often the images of the video bear no relationship to the story of the lyric at all. In either case, something is happening that I believe compromises the integrity of the song and the experience of the listener.

Now we see the music.

As I said earlier in chapter 6, whenever a song is played there are as many versions of that song being heard as there are people listening. This is because we all bring our own catalog of personal experiences to what we are hearing. This results in a sort of audio-prism that colors our interpretation of the song and makes the song uniquely ours.

A music video short-circuits this process.

Imagine you're "listening" to a song. As the music video unfolds, it tells you the song is about a beautiful girl trapped in a shopping mall in another galaxy inhabited by some hideous, undead dancing aliens. Just as it appears she will meet her doom, she is rescued by a handsome guy in neon blue tights with jet propulsion rockets attached to his matching blue helmet. He is the captain of Starship Galleria, patrolling the malls of outer space to rescue beautiful girls from galactic zombie danger.

If you had just *heard* the song, you might have thought it was a song about a relationship; it might have even made you think about *your* relationship.

Not only do music videos short-circuit the personal connection to a song. They also short-circuit imagination. Who knows? Maybe you would have heard the song in the example above and imagined the story taking place in a public library or on a park bench instead of at an intergalactic shopping mall. Whatever the case, it would have been *your* imagination at work.

As it is now, when we watch a music video, we are passively accepting the interpretation of the music video director without giving the song a chance to touch us in a personal way.*

It is for this same reason that people who love to read will not see a movie based on a book until *after* they have read the book. They want to experience the book as originally intended by the author and through the richness of their own imagination. How often have you heard somebody say, "The movie was good, but the book was much better"; or "The movie wasn't nearly as good as the book"? The statement rarely goes the other way.

Translation Unnecessary

When I was in my first year of junior high school in southern California, everyone was required to take at least one music class as part of the basic education requirements. That is how I found myself in a dreary music theory class. As one who already loved all manner of music and had the radio on pretty much all day long when I wasn't in class, I was appalled at how our teacher Ms. Kelly managed to make music the most boring class of the day!

When I was offered the opportunity to transfer out of her class and into orchestra, I jumped at the chance, even though guitarists are usually not needed in an orchestra. Guitar was the only instrument I knew how to play at the time, but that would soon change.

The orchestra teacher, David Winseman—a soft-spoken, scholarly looking man with tinges of gray hair and glasses—took one look at my height and suggested I take up the largest instrument available, the double bass. I went on to play the double bass all through junior high and high school and for one year of college, developing an appreciation and love for classical music in the process.

---

* Music for the Soul has five music videos. Two are performance videos. The other three adhere to the story line of the lyric.

We would always read the sheet music from music stands as we played orchestral pieces, but once we had rehearsed a piece enough times I would often have the bass part memorized. It is then I would close my eyes as we were playing and start to visualize a movie in my own head. From one moment to the next, the vivid music-scapes—alive with drama, pathos, and joy—would send my imagination into overdrive. One minute I was running through the woods; the next I was on the high seas—all without ever leaving the orchestra room.

The same thing was true for me as I grew up listening to the radio. When Billie Joe McAllister jumped off the Tallahatchie Bridge in Bobbie Gentry's "Ode to Billie Joe," I didn't need a music video to see the desperation of his small-town life. I could see "the forty acres left to plow." I could see the sawmill and smell the biscuits. And I got to *imagine* what it was that Billie Joe and his girlfriend threw off the bridge.

Popular radio stations back then played a wide variety of music styles. The balkanization of radio, where a station plays only country or only hip-hop or only rock, had not yet begun. My favorite station at the time, 93-KHJ in Los Angeles, played James Taylor, James Brown, the James Gang, and anyone else who had a great record. This unrestricted access to rock, R & B, folk, fusion, funk, pop, and country helped create a generation with eclectic musical taste and fired the collective imagination!

One of the things I discovered was that not only did songs fire my imagination; they could also perfectly capture a mood. Just ask any Beach Boys fan whether or not their music accurately conveyed the feeling of a summer's day at the beach! The radio I grew up listening to had songs that made you want to dance and shout, songs that made you want to go for a drive with the top down, songs that made you laugh, songs that made you cry; and lots and lots of songs that made you think about the love you were in, the love you just lost, or the love you were looking for.

When I was living on my own in my first apartment, I soon

found that when I was feeling lonely or sad or just needed a good cry, all I had to do was put on the right piece of music. *Appalachian Spring* by Aaron Copland always reduced me to tears. Later on, the soundtracks of Randy Newman would always do the trick, especially *Awakenings* or *Avalon*. As I lay with my eyes closed and listened to these pieces, I could see and feel the emotions without any help from a screen.

Music's ability to evoke emotions and inspire across language barriers has always fascinated me. You don't need to be Russian to be swept up in the passion of Tchaikovsky or German to be moved by Beethoven. Even the addition of lyrics doesn't change this. Two very special experiences that demonstrate the truth of this leap immediately to mind.

> At first we didn't recognize the melody.

The first apartment my wife and I lived in didn't have central air conditioning. Because we were living in southern California at the time, this made for some uncomfortable nights. Our neighborhood included many families from other parts of the world. One unseasonably warm December night we left the windows open. Late in the evening as we were lying in the dark we heard some voices begin singing in a foreign language. The sound was very soothing and reverent. At first we didn't recognize the melody. It dawned on us almost simultaneously. "They're singing 'Silent Night.'" Meredith and I lay in complete stillness wrapped in a blanket of peace. Translation was unnecessary.

Years later at Write About Jesus, a worship band from Hungary sang some original songs in their native tongue. It was a compelling experience. Once again, I found that understanding the words was unnecessary. I was moved by the heart and soul in the music and could feel from the melody, harmony, and rhythm which songs were joyful celebrations of our Lord and those that were songs of reverence.

Neither of these profound experiences included the presence of a video.

The Beautiful People

We are a visual culture now. There is no getting around that. We watch our phones as much or more than we talk on them.

But looks can be deceiving. It is important for us to develop discernment in assessing the barrage of images that come our way.

Nowhere is this more true than with the myriad of images, possibly up to 5,000 per day![1]—many of them doctored—that are being marketed to people in their teens and twenties. That message, that you too can be, and *should* be, one of the Beautiful People, comes in various forms of advertising, both overt and subtle.

But perhaps most influential is the hyper-sexualized content of a large percentage of music videos. When the first music videos came on the scene in the sixties, it was impossible to imagine the extent to which they would come to glorify causal sex and misogyny. When "It's Hard Out Here for a Pimp" won the Oscar for Best Song in 2005, it was a clear signal that such messaging in song had gone "mainstream."

As one who has devoted his life to the proposition that a song is the greatest from of communication on the face of the earth, you can imagine how deeply troubling I find the popularity of artists whose careers are built on self-aggrandizing hedonism and songs that routinely degrade women and portray them in lyrics and in videos as objects to be used, rather than human beings to be cherished. I believe this grieves the heart of God.

Because a song can get into one's brain and become a tape loop, replaying again and again, I felt God calling Music for the Soul to create a music project dealing with the subject of eating disorders and body image. I learned just how devastating this can be for young people, and especially for girls, while working on the *Tell Me What You See* project. The pervasive message that thinner, younger, and beautiful is better is coming in loud and clear—and is doing cataclysmic damage to the psyche of women. In turn, many are harming themselves physically and engaging in self-injurious behaviors in an effort to fit into an unattainable mold.

The motivations and methods of self-deception involved with body image and eating disorders are incredibly complex. To do the project justice I needed expertise far beyond my education and experience. Many times in ministry I've been told that "God doesn't call the equipped. He equips the called." That's how it felt with *Tell Me What You See*. God graciously provided relationships with people who were able to speak knowledgeably and with wisdom into what type of content was needed for the project.

Dr. Linda Mintle,[2] author of *Making Peace with Your Thighs* and *Press Pause Before You Eat*, helped me understand the root problems behind struggles with food. Dr. Gregg Jantz,[3] founder of The Center in Edmonds, Washington, and author of *Hope, Help, & Healing for Eating Disorders* and *Living Beyond Food* was also tremendously helpful to me during the process of creating the CD.

As work progressed on *Tell Me What You See*, I began to feel that it would be important for listeners who were struggling with body image issues to hear the message from those who had lived it. Accordingly, I turned to several of the young female Christian songwriters I knew who had a personal relationship with the issue to contribute songs for the project.

Sara Beth Geoghegan came to my house one day and played a song called "Beautiful Jesus" that took my breath away. It was infused with heartbreaking honesty. It was a life raft of hope. When she finished it she turned to me with tears in her eyes and said, "Do you think this song could ever help anybody?"

"Sara Beth, I think this song is going to save somebody's life," I replied.

> *She looks in the mirror several times a day*
> *And each time she's wishing that what she sees will change*
> *And she blames God for making her that way*

And now she's comparing to what she thinks the best
Her thoughts so consuming they leave her without rest
What a lovely mess
She lies down on the floor
She cannot take anymore

Beautiful Jesus
Make me look like You
Beautiful Jesus
I'm dying to be truly beautiful
Make me look like You[4]

What Does God See?

I spent several months researching, thinking, and praying about the insidious nature of eating disorders. What must it be like to feel as if one's own body is the enemy to the point where self-deprivation or self-harm might seem like a solution?

Then at 4:00 a.m. one morning I woke up. The thoughts would not let me sleep. I grabbed a yellow legal pad and a pencil and went for a walk in the dark. Soon a lyric started to come. I paused underneath streetlights to scribble down the lines. The sun was just beginning to come up when I came back to my house with the lyric to "The Cost" in hand.

Wanting to be sure that the words I'd written authentically conveyed the lived experience of someone with an eating disorder, I called my friend Constance Rhodes later that day and read them to her. Constance is the author of *Life Inside the Thin Cage* and *The Art of Being* and is founder and director of FINDINGbalance,[5] a ministry that helps people find health and freedom in their relationship with food. She assured me that the lyrics accurately communicated the emotions a disordered eater feels.

With the lyric in place, I then reached out to the superbly talented Missi Hale to write the music. The song captures the illusion of control that can "empower" a disordered eater.

> *They can't make me eat if I don't want to*
> *They can't make me keep it down if I don't want to*
> *They can't live inside me*
> *They can't deny me*
> *Control*
> *Sweet control*[6]

By the end of the song the protagonist is asking herself, "Who's in control?" The music and vocal performance mirror the collapse of her illusions. At first she is arrogant, even cocky. As the song moves forward, the music becomes increasingly disquieting, as she is unable to assimilate her conflicting emotions. Finally the music track and the vocal track both come apart completely, dissolving to reflect that her coping mechanisms are no longer sufficient.

Allie Lapointe's lyrics to the title track, "Tell Me What You See," brought home the important truth that it is God's opinion that should matter the most to each of us. The world—and sometimes our own families and friends and even *ourselves*—will tell us that we are not smart enough, not rich enough, and not good looking enough. The question we need to ask is what does God see when He looks upon us—those who have been created in God's very image (see Genesis 1:26).

> *You say I am Your masterpiece*
> *Your artwork, Your design*
> *Yet I've questioned every brushstroke*
> *And altered all the lines*

With every gain and every loss
My vision blurs with tears
Until I can't see anything
Past the stranger in the mirror
I don't recognize myself
I'm desperate for Your help, so . . .

Will You draw my portrait
And tell me what You see?
Will You shine Your light of truth
On the real me?
I can't see fact from fiction
And I long for clarity
So tell me what You see
Tell me what You see[7]

First Samuel 16:7 says, "People look at the outward appearance, but the LORD looks at the heart." This suggests that the clarity we long for—and the deep emotional well-being we long for—is not to be found by focusing on the surface.

A hairstyle, a makeover, new shoes—all these kinds of things can make us feel better in the moment, and they may even constitute good self-care on occasion. But they will never bring us the peace in our soul that comes from knowing our Creator loves us just as we are.

This is not only a female issue. Men worry about their expanding waistlines and contracting hairlines. Many worry about maintaining a youthful appearance to not lose out on a job to a younger-looking competitor.

There is nothing wrong with exercise and eating a proper diet. In fact these are good and important things. There's not even anything wrong with getting a hair transplant. But all of these are secondary to the condition of our souls.

In 1994 I wrote a never-recorded song called "The Promise Is You" with Brian Barrett, a Starsong recording artist. The song contains a brilliant line of his that I never forgot: "The sweetest frame will bend with age." I've thought about that line many times as I see stories about people trying to hold back the hands of times with repeated Botox injections and plastic surgeries. Prioritizing and fixating on our appearance can, at best, bring us only temporary happiness. Until we are able to accept ourselves and love ourselves as we are, a healthy sense of self will always be elusive.

God loves you just as you are.

The song that was playing when I decided to follow Jesus with my life was "Just as I Am." Written by Charlotte Elliott in 1835, the essence of the lyric is that we don't have to wait to stop being sinners before we come before God. The fourth stanza echoes essentially what Sara Beth's "Beautiful Jesus" says—that focusing on God, and not on ourselves, is where our hope is found.

> *Just as I am—poor, wretched, blind;*
> *Sight, riches, healing of the mind,*
> *Yea, all I need, in Thee to find,*
> *O Lamb of God, I come!*

But doesn't this also apply to appearance? God loves you just as you are. This is *very* good news. It was certainly good news for me as a teenager, agonizing over a bad complexion. It means you don't have to embody any particular culture's definition of physical beauty to become acceptable in the eyes of God. And if it is good enough for God, then shouldn't it be good enough for us?

After the release of *Tell Me What You See*, we received a letter that described, yet again, how a song can play a meaningful role in someone's life. In it were these words: "This is my tool that I play for my husband when I can't explain why I don't want him to touch me. I play it for my mother when I can't explain why I can't give up my workouts." What a blessing to hear that the recording could help bridge the communication gap for someone with an eating disorder and their family.

Another response from a young woman who had found freedom from her eating disorder affirmed this thought: "I wish my family could have listened to this CD while I was going through anorexia. It would have given us a place to start in conversation and would have given me words for the things I couldn't bring myself to speak about my addictions and control issues, and how [my family] could help me."

These responses and others like them remind me that God has given us the gift of songs as one way to deal with topics and feelings that can sometimes seem too difficult to address. Why? . . .

Three reasons: First, a song can give us a place to start when we don't know where to begin. Second, a song can often say the very thing we want to say better than we could express it ourselves. And third, in a song, the music can set a healing, emotional tone, providing a comforting context for an uncomfortable conversation.

A softened heart has more capacity to respond to a hard situation. And it has been my experience time and time again that music can and does touch and soften our hearts.

When that happens healing can begin—because a softened heart has more capacity to respond to the love of God our Creator, the One who desires greater wholeness and freedom for us all.

Songs from Tell Me What You See *can be streamed at www.musicforthesoul.org/resources/ tell-me-what-you-see.*

14

JUST ONE SONG

"Every moment in the river has its song."
MICHAEL JACKSON

Before individual songs were available on the Internet, record companies used to release "singles" and promote them to get airplay on radio stations. If a recording artist could have a "hit" on the radio—a song that was being played everywhere and often—then that would drive people into the record stores where they could buy the album that had the single on it. Record companies often released several singles from one album. The more hit singles, the higher the sales of that particular album were likely to be.

By the late 1960s, the average album had about twenty minutes of music time per side. Having forty minutes to work with gave artists the opportunity to share about ten to twelve songs per album. Rather than having just ten random songs, the most innovative artists used the album format as a canvas to tell a larger story. The album itself became an art form. Each song became a part of the whole. Context mattered, with every song having additional impact because of its relationship to the others.

Several of the most-enduring albums of the next several years were concept albums—recordings like the Beatles' *Sgt. Pepper's Lonely Hearts Club Band*, the Who's *Tommy*, and Pink Floyd's *The*

Wall. Others, though not concept albums per se, carried a theme throughout in the mood they created, such as with Joni Mitchell's landmark recording *Blue.*

In the ministry of Music for the Soul, we've created a lot of full-length projects. In a sense, each one of them is a concept album—dealing in depth with a particular path of healing relating to one specific topic. Because healing is a process, we've found that placing songs within such a framework is helpful. In that way each song is better understood as it relates to the overall process.

Lines began coming fast, one after the other.

But every once in awhile there has come an opportunity to write a song meant to convey one key truth for which no additional context seems necessary. Such was the opportunity with the song "Child of God."

A number of people from Salvation Army locations around the country had been ordering *Somebody's Daughter.* I wanted to find out why so I called the Salvation Army national office in Washington, DC, to see what might be behind this. The trail led to Lisa Thompson. At that time Thompson was serving as the Liaison for the Abolition of Sexual Trafficking.* It turned out that Lisa thought very highly of *Somebody's Daughter* and had encouraged others within the organization to use it.

As we talked, Lisa shared more with me about her passion for those who were being sex trafficked. I told her that I would be interested in trying to write a song about the issue and asked her to send me any material she might have that would help me understand the issue more fully. She obliged, and in just a few days I had pages and pages of information as well as several compelling first-person stories of women who had been trafficked for sexual purposes.

---

* She is now Director of Education and Outreach for the National Center on Sexual Exploitation.

As I sat down to read some of the stories, I had a visceral response, literally turning some of the pages over because the words were too painful to read. I wanted to reject the idea that any human being could possibly use another human being in such a reprehensible and dehumanizing fashion. But almost immediately the thought came to me, *If these women have had the courage and fortitude to live these stories, the least I can do is have the guts to read them.*

And so I pressed on. For several weeks I ruminated on these stories and continued to learn more about the issue of sex trafficking both by reading about it and through conversations with those who had experienced it. Then one day, when I was in the drive-through line at the bank—not thinking about the issue or a song at all—lyric lines began coming fast, one after the other.

I paint on the face
Strap on the heels
Shut down my heart
so it won't have to feel
The hands that don't know me
all over my skin
and the eyes that don't love me
drinking me in[1]

I quickly pulled my car out of the line and drove as fast as I could to the nearest church where I knew there was a piano available. The following day I sent the song to Lisa to see if she felt it captured the message. "It's like you have walked in the shoes of a prostituted woman," was her response.

Normally it takes a long time for budgets to come together, but the financing to record "Child of God" came nearly as quickly as the song had itself. My friend Bonnie Pritchard, who also lives in the DC area and has worked as an anti-trafficking advocate, had been working on a project with singer Pat Boone. She had spoken with him about the trafficking issue. She felt that he would have an interest in what we were doing and called him. That very same afternoon Boone and I were on the phone.

In the fifties, Boone, a handsome heartthrob with a smooth vocal style, became well known to a generation of parents as the safe alternative to that leather-wearing, hip-shaking renegade Elvis Presley. No powder puff himself, Boone went on to sell nearly fifty million records and had thirty-eight top-ten singles. He is in the top ten of highest-selling recording artists of all time. He became an Academy-award-winning songwriter in 1959 when he wrote the lyric of the theme song for the movie *Exodus*.

Pat's entrance into this story requires a brief side trip in the Way Back machine.

In 1967 I was called into principal Betty Freeman's office at Dixie Canyon Elementary School. I figured I must have done something wrong though I had no idea what it was. It turns out a representative from *The Pat Boone Show*, then a half-hour morning program on NBC television, had come to interview potential guests for Boone's show. They were planning a segment on the program where they were going to interview kids, and Mrs. Freeman had selected me as one of the children to be interviewed.

At the time my family had a row of tomato plants growing all along the back fence in the yard of our Studio City, California, home. As a result I had quite a crop of tomato worms. Now, if you've never seen a tomato worm, let me tell you; they look like something straight out of a bad horror movie. They are light green with what look like eyeballs all along the sides of their bodies and have an orange horn protruding from one end. Anyway, I prattled on and on about my tomato worms. Apparently the guest coordinator found this to be potentially compelling television, and I was chosen to be on the show.

By the time the day came for the show taping, all of my worms had died, and I remember standing frozen like a statue in my little blue velour pullover and giving poor Pat a string of monosyllabic answers. Recounting this story to Pat forty years later made for a great icebreaker when we spoke.

Anyway, Boone and I talked for a while on the phone about the seriousness of the sex-trafficking issue, how the song had come to be written, and our recording plans. He asked what the budget was and agreed without hesitation to cover the recording costs. Not a powder puff indeed!

The Right Vocalist

With our budget in hand, I began to think about who the right vocalist for the project might be. I wanted someone with a soulful, bluesy style and a vocal tone with some edge to it—a sound that might be suggestive of having lived through some difficult experiences. Immediately Danielle Reed* came to mind.

I called Danielle, and she agreed to sing the song for us. The day of the session we met at Kent Hooper's studio, the House of Big in Franklin, Tennessee. It was just the three of us—Kent, Danielle, and myself. The usual process for this kind of session is that the singer sits down and listens through the track, a lyric sheet in hand, while I sing through the melody. The singer makes some notations on the lyric sheet and gradually begins to sing along, as he or she learns the song. Danielle, a consummate professional, is a quick study and had the song down in short order.

Once the singer goes into the vocal booth, the recording engineer tries out some different microphones and some different settings on the recording equipment until he is pleased with the sound. Kent is an expert at this.

After the microphone and settings are selected, recording begins. Generally the first few takes are more like practice. However, with a

---

* Not her real name

great singer like Danielle, you want to make sure you are recording from the very first take because if you don't something very special may be lost forever.

As Danielle was singing I had a lyric sheet with a grid on it so that I could mark the takes that I liked the best. For example, 2nd line from take 1, 4th line from take 2, lines 5 through 7 from take 3—and so on. By recording this way after several performances have been captured, one can then put together one performance including all of the best takes. This is called "comping."

After a dozen or so passes, the coverage on my sheet was pretty thorough, and I called Danielle back into the control room to hear a playback. She listened intently, and when the song was finished she said shook her head. "I'm not her yet," she said, referring to the character in the song and turned and headed back into the vocal booth.

Danielle then proceeded to blister the track from top to bottom with a vocal full of raw emotion and power. There would be no need for comping on this day.

Danielle came back into the control room and sat down on the sofa. She seemed to be reflecting on something. "You guys don't know my story, do you?" she asked quietly. We didn't.

"This week I'm going to meet my dad for the very first time. Only he's not going to know it's me," she said. Then after a pause, "He raped my mom."

Kent and I were stunned. After my initial shock and sadness over the fact that this was a part of Danielle's story, something else began to dawn on me.

In my research of the sex-trafficking issue, I had seen interviews with young women who were being sold over and over and over again in the course of one day. It occurred to me now that these women were going to hear a song written about their lives sung by a woman whose mother was a victim of sexual assault.

This was no coincidence. I felt that somehow, in God's ongoing work of reconciliation, the trafficked women—all children of God—would feel a special connection to Danielle's voice as being their own. I had not known Danielle's story when I called her to sing this song. But God did.

With the lead vocal in hand, we next scheduled the background vocal session. Fittingly, the choir was recorded in the large room at Oceanway Studio A in Nashville—formerly a church sanctuary.

"I'm not her yet."

When the entire recording was completed, I sent the song to Lisa Thompson who shared it through her vast network of colleagues working on the issue of sex trafficking around the world. We heard from those on the front lines and from trafficking survivors themselves in places like Chile, Sweden, Canada, Trinidad, and from all over the United States.

A young woman helping sex-trafficked girls in Northeast China wrote us this note: "As a woman delivered from a lifestyle of four years [of] prostitution in the United States I am so thankful for the raw truth of your song 'Child of God'! It truly does speak right to the heart of where I was at that time in my life. I talk with young women all the time in schools all around the world and often hear their stories of being prostituted or sexually abused, etc. I will use your song when speaking to these young people."

Another woman told me that she had been trafficked earlier in her life. She said that every line of the first verse was exactly her experience, except for the reference to wearing high heels. "I wore sneakers," she told me, "in case I had to run."

Renee Is Fourteen

Ironically, I had unknowingly written a song about sex trafficking long before anyone was even calling it that. One day in 1984 while living in Los Angeles, I read a heartrending article in the *LA*

Times. It was a story about a young girl who had run away from an abusive home environment in Kansas. It seems that this fourteen-year-old had hitched a ride to southern California simply because she figured if she was going to be homeless she should go where the weather was warm. Within only a few short weeks she was being prostituted on the streets of Hollywood.

I couldn't get this girl's story out of my mind and wound up writing a song about her entitled "Renee Is Fourteen." For many years it was a song I would play at writers' nights where songwriters share their songs. Eventually it was recorded by my friend Rick Altizer.

> "Everything that happened in that song happened to *me*."

On one occasion a schoolteacher used the song as an exercise in compassion with her class. She had the students listen to the song and then had each of them write a letter to Renee as if she were a real person. She mounted all the letters on a trifold display board and sent it to me. I deeply appreciated her sharing with me the moving letters her students had written. It was a blessing to see the way Renee's story had touched their hearts.

After that I didn't think much about the song, only occasionally sharing it with new friends. Then in 2009 something extraordinary happened.

My friend Shelly Beach is an author, a caregiver, and a healer. She had just begun consulting with me on the creation of the *Dignity* project for caregivers. Shelly's very nature is to listen to people's hearts and to offer them encouragement and hope. And she is a big believer in the power of a song to help in that process. In preparing for her consulting role, she had spent some time listening to my catalogue to familiarize herself with my work.

Shelly does a lot of radio interviews to promote the books she writes. She had recently been on a Christian radio program based out of San Francisco and felt a prompting in her spirit to call the show's producer Wanda Sanchez, whom she had only previously communicated with through e-mail. She did a little research on Facebook and discovered that Sanchez had an interest in inner-city missions.

For a few weeks Shelly argued with God about whether or not to call the producer to whom she had never spoken a word. Finally, she e-mailed Wanda and suggested a "Get to know you" call. Wanda replied to the e-mail and made it clear that she did *not* want to make friends. That is when Shelly got the bright idea to send another e-mail to Wanda pitching me for a guest shot on the program.

Just a few weeks earlier I'd sent Shelly a copy of "Renee Is Fourteen." Shelly thought the song might be meaningful to Wanda because of her interest in inner-city missions so she attached a copy of the song to the e-mail. She also included a song called "Every Single Tear," about how God sees and cares about every single tear we cry, and another called "Dead Hearts Don't Cry," about sexual abuse.

Upon getting up the next morning, Wanda opened her e-mail to find the three songs sitting in her inbox. After listening she called Shelly. When Shelly answered the phone, Wanda immediately started screaming at her. "Why did you send me these songs?" she angrily demanded.

Shelly fumbled for an explanation, saying that she thought since Wanda had a heart for inner-city missions she must know some of the "Renees" in the world and probably had compassion for them.

Wanda responded by breaking into tears and saying, "I *am* Renee! This is *my* story. I ran away when I was fourteen. Everything that happened in that song happened to *me*."

Shelly was taken aback. But even though Wanda remained defensive at first, Shelly kept talking and gradually learned more of the horrific story of abuse and pain that had led Wanda to the brink of suicide in recent days.

As they talked more, it became clear to Shelly that something in those songs had touched Wanda in a deep place, enabling her to talk to a total stranger about things that she had kept hidden from her closest friends—and even from herself—for years and years. The songs had put her unspeakable story into words, made her feel known and understood. They had given voice to her pain through the poignant melodies in a way that she could not have done for herself. And once the damn burst, there was no putting the pain away again.

Wanda began telling Shelly more and more about her nightmarish past, which included verbal, physical, and sexual abuse. As Shelly heard each new piece of the story, she became convicted in her heart that she needed to help Wanda build upon this fragile new hope she had found.

Shelly sent her more songs from the Music for the Soul catalog that spoke to the wounded child inside of Wanda with a language of love, approval, and belonging. And she committed to walk with her as a friend first through long, often difficult, phone conversations and later on in person.

Ultimately, with Shelly's help, Wanda was able to take the step of seeking counseling and to continue on a deeper path to healing. Shelly told me that without the songs it would have never been possible. "God used your songs to tell Wanda her own story," she said. "That led her to seek help."

Remarkably, Wanda lives in victory today using the story of overcoming the trauma in her life to help others who are struggling to make peace with the trauma in their past. She and Shelly have written a wonderful book[2] together and tour the country speaking to and blessing women in prisons, churches, and at conferences.

A Wonderful Idea

Another single song opportunity came years earlier when Doug Shaw, the gentleman I met in a cab, and I were having a conversation about the deployment of American soldiers to Iraq. "It would be great if you wrote a song to encourage the families of those who are separated from a loved one due to military service."

I thought his suggestion was a wonderful idea, and I brought it up to Scott Krippayne and Tony Wood during our next scheduled writing session. The song that resulted was "Prayer for You." The song reflects the pain of the separation from both perspectives, the soldier and his or her family.

Half my heart is half a world away
It feels like the life in me is missing
From the moment I awake
I put on my brave face
and fight back the tears that want to flow
it almost hurts me more to hear your voice
'cause it makes me want to feel your arms around me
We ache across the miles
We have to for awhile
but still there is hope

I'm sending out a prayer for you
Knowing that you're praying too
While we're living in this loneliness
We can trust
the God that we're both looking to
is looking out for us[3]

Since the deployment was already happening, we wanted to make the song available as soon as possible. There was a studio for recording demos right down the hall from Tony's office at the publishing company so we went there, and Scott recorded a quick piano/vocal version of the song. With that in hand, I put it on the Music for the Soul website and started letting my contacts in the Christian music world know that the song was available if they were looking for anything to encourage military families.

The song touched a chord.

This approach, not much of a marketing strategy, worked much better than I had expected it would. Within just a matter of days, the song was being played on eighteen Christian radio stations and was in heavy rotation on a pair of stations in Florida and Minnesota. It worked so well, in fact, that it actually wound up causing some confusion.

Spring Hill, Scott's record company, had recently released a single to radio from his new album *It Goes like This*. Radio station personnel were calling to ask, "Which one of these Scott Krippayne songs is the new single?" The fact that they would think a simple piano/vocal demo was the real single was a testament to Scott's compelling vocal performance.

Being able to respond quickly to a situation is one of the advantages of being a small, not-for-profit organization. The song touched a chord with many who were being separated by deployment.

One woman shared, "It is amazing how you captured what it is like to have a spouse over there on the other side of the world preparing for war. So many things mentioned in the song are things that I have shared with my mother or a close friend."

Another woman said, "As the wife of a recently deployed soldier, these words express *exactly* how I feel."

For another wife it had lasting impact. "I heard 'Prayer for You' when we lived in Florida and my husband was deployed for months at a time. I'll never forget—I was driving, it was raining, the song came on 'out of the blue' and it couldn't have hit my heart any harder. I've never forgotten it, and there has been no other song like it to relate the feelings we experience all too often."

The ability to address an anxiety-filled event, such as a forced separation, is yet another example of the power of a song to bring comfort and affirmation for those experiencing life's deepest, most challenging emotions.

Set Free

An opportunity soon followed that was perhaps an even more profound challenge. I had been co-writer and co-executive producer on a CD and video project entitled *David: Ordinary Man, Extraordinary God* for Discovery House music. The album was to be performed live in St. Paul, Minnesota, at the University of Northwestern Minnesota.

During my time in St. Paul, I had the opportunity to meet a woman named Maureen Magnusson. She shared with me some incredible stories about praying with women who had profound pain and sadness from an abortion in their past. It was deeply moving to hear how the healing power of prayer was helping these women.

Upon returning to Nashville, I spoke with several other women about this issue and then contacted Dwight Liles and asked him if he would help me work on a song based on what Maureen had shared with me. The song "We Forgive You," a song sung from the perspective of Jesus, was the result.

Since there was no full-length project for abortion-wounded hearts on the Music for the Soul schedule at that time, I decided we should find a way to share this song in the short term as soon as possible. I asked Sue Foster in our office to do some research, and she came up with a list of Christian crisis pregnancy centers and support groups all around the country. We then e-mailed a simple piano/vocal version of the song free to more than four hundred organizations around the country.

We received e-mails, calls, and letters of thanks from Florida to California; however, we were in for a couple of surprising responses—ways that the song was to be used—that were firsts for us!

The first was from a group called the Life Ballet in Rochester, New York. Sandy Arena, the director of the troupe, had abortion as part of her story. She asked for permission to incorporate the song into their live dance performances. It was breathtaking to see the emotion of the song expressed through dance!

Then we heard from a memorial garden especially for children who had been lost to abortion. They asked for permission to put the lyrics to the song on a monument in the garden.

And in one of the most touching responses we have received, we heard from a woman named Paula Ellefson who leads a ministry called Rich in Mercy in Rochester, Minnesota. She does a memorial service for those who have lost a child due to an abortion decision. As part of the service, they write the name of the child on a card and light a candle in the child's honor. She told me that they played "We Forgive You" during this service. "Everyone was totally blessed by it," she shared. "Some said it was as though it came straight from heaven! There were tears shed and one woman said, 'I felt the shame just fall off of me and I was released and set free!'"

There is no greater joy than to hear that a song we shared has been a part of helping someone experience the healing and renewing forgiveness of Jesus Christ.

Not long after writing "We Forgive You," I received a phone call from my friend 'Nita Whitaker. Nita is an extremely talented vocalist based in Los Angeles. She and her husband Don were supporters of an organization called the Starkey Hearing Foundation that provides hearing aids for children in impoverished countries who could otherwise not afford them. They were looking for a theme song and wanted to know if I would be interested in co-writing the song with 'Nita.

As someone who has spent his life receiving joy and meaning from using his ears—listening to and working with music—I felt like God was giving me an incredible opportunity to give back. I was honored to accept!

Once the Starkey Foundation heard the completed song, they invited 'Nita to sing it at their annual fund-raising event taking place in St. Paul, Minnesota. To call it an event is an understatement. It was extraordinary!

"I felt the shame just fall off of me."

The evening started off with a silent auction that included sports memorabilia such as basketball superstar Shaquille O'Neal's shoes and a ball autographed by New York Yankee baseball legend Babe Ruth. Beautiful artwork, exotic vacations, and many other high-value items were offered. After that, a crowd of about a thousand—including many television, film, and sports celebrities—was ushered into a large ballroom for dinner and a program.

Early in the evening 'Nita delivered a beautiful, soaring rendition of our song set to a video showing some of the children who were helped by receiving hearing aids. Later, I was thoroughly surprised when special guest performer Sir Elton John was introduced!

The evening successfully raised $2.7 million for the work of the foundation. It was an honor for Music for the Soul to be part of helping such a worthwhile cause.

We later partnered with Douglas Shaw & Associates on a song called "Days of Hope," which rescue missions in Cleveland, Milwaukee, and several other locations across the country used to address the issue of homelessness in their communities.

But perhaps the single song project for which I have been the most grateful is one that happened very early on in the life of the ministry. It was in 2002, and the attacks from 9/11 were still painfully present in everyone's mind. A woman named Joyce Boaz, director of an organization called Gift from Within, contacted me. She was working with police officers suffering from post-traumatic stress and asked me if Music for the Soul could provide a song to help.

I asked her if she could send me some case studies, which she did. I read first-person accounts from several police officers, each describing harrowing experiences encountered in their normal course of duty. It was hard to imagine a person living through any of these types of incidents and then trying to go about life as if nothing out of the ordinary had happened.

It helped that during the previous few years I'd become friends with a police sergeant with whom I attended church. Getting to know and love Don Adcox had already sensitized me to the fact the police officers are people with real families and hopes and dreams, not just the people who pulled me over when my license plate tags were expired.

For many weeks I ruminated on the stories Joyce had sent me. Then one morning the idea came to me that perhaps there was a way we could help officers who heard the song to feel known and understood—and pay tribute to them at the same time. "Heroes Unsung" was the result. As I began working on the lyric, images of officers running *into* danger rather than away from it were fresh in my mind.

> *Without a thought for yourselves*
> *You race into the fires of hell*
> *Unselfishly you sacrifice*
> *and give your all to save a life*
> *Anonymity's a pale reward*
> *for all the things you've done*
> *Heroes unsung*

You've seen the worst the world can give
You hold inside what you can't forget
The armor grows to block the pain
It's just so hard to communicate
And you never thought that you'd burn out
But sometimes you feel numb
Heroes unsung

With uncommon acts of bravery
You rush into harm's way
Giving something to the rest of us
There is no way to repay
Have we taken you for granted
Without counting up the cost
'cause every time we lose even one of you
The best of us is lost[4]

One evening after having recorded the song, the phone rang just as my family and I were getting ready to go out to dinner. It was a woman named Beverly Anderson from the Metropolitan Police Employee Assistance Program in Washington, DC. She was calling to invite Music for the Soul to present "Heroes Unsung" at the annual Peace Officers Memorial Day service, which was to be held at the United States Capitol. The audience of ten thousand would be made up of police officers and their families.

Much prayer and soul searching goes into beginning a ministry. Even after starting, one is continuously seeking God's leading and—I can only speak for myself—looking for affirmation. There is much second-guessing, questioning, and, of course, prayer. "Lord, is this what *You* want me to be doing?"

So when Music for the Soul's first public appearance ever turned out to be on the U.S. Capitol lawn following a speech by

President George W. Bush, you can imagine I literally pinched myself. I can remember thinking, *As affirmations go, this is a doozy.*

Later on, I received several responses from officers, like this letter from Kevin, a police officer from Virginia. "When I heard the song, it made me realize that somebody really knows what I am going through. I don't feel alone anymore."

Although I was incredibly gratified by all of the feedback we received, it was a response from my friend Larry that rocked me.

During the Viet Nam War, Larry had been a fighter pilot and befriended two other pilots. All three of them were newly married when they went overseas. Only Larry came home.

Over lunch he described to me how he had carried guilt over the years for being the only one of the three to have survived the war. *Why me?* he had wondered over and over again. He told me that as he listened to "Heroes Unsung" he had broken down and wept for his friends and for himself. "I felt the presence of God as I listened. Not in some remote way, but in a very powerful way."

Once again I was moved by God's ability to take a song and minister "out of context," using a piece written for police officers to minister to a man carrying a painful wartime memory. It was a deeply humbling experience.

Of course songs have been used successfully to help with many good humanitarian causes throughout the years. In addition to the aforementioned "We Are the World," which raised money for the hungry in Africa, there have been several others: "Do They Know It's Christmas" raised money to fight poverty in Ethiopia; "That's What Friends Are For" raised money for AIDS research; and more recently, Taylor Swift's "Ronan" raised money for cancer research—just to name a few.

As you can see, the width and breadth of issues that songs can tackle effectively knows no bounds. Because of their ability to equally engage the intellect and the emotions, songs will always be a uniquely effective means of caring for hurting minds and wounded hearts.

What better way to share the hope and compassion of Christ?

"Child of God" can be streamed at www.musicforthesoul.org/resources/child-of-god.

"Renee Is Fourteen" can be streamed at www.musicforthesoul.org/resources/broken-to-bless.

"Prayer for You" can be streamed at www.musicforthesoul.org/resources/prayer-for-you.

"Days of Hope" can be streamed at www.musicforthesoul.org/resources/days-of-hope.

"Heroes Unsung" an be streamed at www. musicforthesoul.org/resources/heroes-unsung.

15

A Companion on the Journey

"Who hears music feels his solitude peopled at once."
ROBERT BROWNING

In 2007 I received a call from a woman named Carmen Leal. She was the author of a book called *The Twenty-Third Psalm for Caregivers*. She had heard Anita Lustrea interviewing me on Moody Radio Network's program *Midday Connection*. We had been talking about "Twenty-Three," the Music for the Soul version of the beloved Scripture set to music. Carmen was putting together a conference for caregivers and wanted to know if I would come and lead the worship music.

As one who'd never led worship at even a small church before, I felt completely unqualified, but Carmen was very persuasive. When she told me the name of the conference, "Someone Cares," I laughed and said, "I think we may have already written your theme song." Sure enough, when Carmen heard "Someone Who Cares," a song written by Scott Krippayne and myself several years earlier, she decided it would make a great theme song for the conference.[1] I was interested in learning more about caregiving, a new topic to me at the time, and the conference was taking place at Ridgecrest

Conference Center in beautiful Asheville, North Carolina. I decided to walk through this door of opportunity that God was opening. It was a life-changing experience.

At the conference I witnessed selfless, Christlike love in action. I heard story after story from courageous people who'd sacrificed everything to provide the kind of love and care they believed their loved ones deserved. I also heard from professional caregivers who became a lifeline for the ones they served and came to love them in the process.

But no one affected me as deeply as Dick and Elizabeth.

Dignity through Love

Elizabeth had been the kind of schoolteacher who was every kid's favorite. She was vibrant, energetic, creative, and fun, a real hands-on kind of a lady. Not only was she that way during the week; she was also a mother to three children of her own and a beloved Sunday school teacher.

She and Dick enjoyed being active together, often taking long walks in the woods. Then they both began to notice that something wasn't right. A creeping fear tugged at their hearts, as they had to admit that Elizabeth was having trouble doing some of the things she had always done effortlessly. It wasn't long before they received the diagnosis. Elizabeth had a progressive form of multiple sclerosis.

The lady who had done so much for so many gradually lost the ability to do even the most mundane tasks for herself. She fought it with everything she had, but eventually it was Dick who was brushing her hair, Dick who was feeding her her meals, and Dick who was helping her in the bathroom.

I remember thinking, *Where is the dignity?* as I tried to imagine how hard it must be for Elizabeth. After so many years of being an active mother and a teacher, she now was unable to care for herself, let alone for others.

Even as Dick shared this heartbreaking story, it was clear that he adored his wife, and though he would have never chosen this path, he was glad to be able to provide the loving care she needed. And her love for him was evident in her eyes as they sat side by side.

When I got home from the weekend, I wanted to create a song to honor Dick and Elizabeth and the many other incredible care-givers I had met. I prayerfully asked for God's guidance. The song "Dignity" was the result.

The following year I was invited to do the music for the con-ference again and began the music time with "Dignity." No sooner had the piano fallen silent than someone in the audience called out, "Play it again!" I did. Then later, as I was coming down off the stage, Carmen whispered to me, "Play 'Dignity' again tomorrow." In that moment I felt that God had answered my prayer. Written from the perspective of the care receiver, the song says in part:

> *I look in your eyes*
> *and to my surprise*
> *When you look at me*
> *You see more than a disease*
> *It's by your caring*
> *That I am getting through*
> *You have been Jesus*
> *When only He would do*
> *When this is hard*
> *Know deep in your heart*
> *The gift that you've given to me*
> *That gift is nothing less*
> *Than my dignity[2]*

Knowing that Carmen had lovingly cared for a husband with a severe disability for many years, and knowing Dick and Elizabeth's story, made the issue personal for me. But, as I started to do the research, I was overwhelmed by the millions of people living out a similar story. One morning as we sat in our living room, my wife told me she believed a project to encourage caregivers was what Music for the Soul should do next.

Ambushed by Grace

No sooner had my wife made her pronouncement than the miracles started happening, such as the first time I met my friend Shelly Beach. I was doing a radio interview with Lesley Hurst on her program *Vocal Point*, which emanated from Ft. Lauderdale, Florida. We were talking about the new song "Child of God" that Music for the Soul had just released on the topic of sex trafficking. During a commercial break I heard Lesley doing a promo, saying, "Tomorrow's guest will be Shelly Beach, author of a book called *Ambushed by Grace* on the subject of caregiving." After our interview was over, I asked Lesley if I could have Shelly Beach's phone number since we were getting ready to work on a project for caregivers. Lesley gave me Shelly's contact info in Michigan.

I immediately called Shelly on her cell and told her why I was calling. I began to tell her about the Music for the Soul ministry. She said, "You're not going to believe this. I'm on my way to a film festival to see a screening of your DVD *Somebody's Daughter*. One of the cameramen for the project goes to my church!"

Shelly agreed to send me *Ambushed by Grace* and a devotional book she had written for caregivers entitled *Precious Lord, Take My Hand*.

Over the next several months I came to understand that God had gone before me and made all the connections to bless me with the perfect consultant to address every angle of caregiving. Shelly had provided care in her home for her mother with Alzheimer's, her father-in-law with Parkinson's disease, and her father with dementia. She had also been a care receiver when she had experienced a brain malady that left her bedridden for several months. Between her personal experience, her two wonderful books, and her incredible nurturing heart, Shelly was a wellspring of caregiving knowledge and a wonderful partner to shepherd the content for the *Dignity* CD.

> My subconscious had been at work on a song.

Next came a songwriting miracle.

I've written thousands of songs through the years. They come in all kinds of ways. Sometimes the music comes first, and sometimes the lyrics come first. Sometimes they come together. As a rule of thumb it generally helps to be awake, but even that is not always necessary. Sometimes I wake up with a lyric being birthed. Sometimes I wake up with a melody rattling around in my head.

But *never*—not in over thirty years of writing songs—had I ever awakened with the lyric and the music already joined together. Such was the way that "We've Never Done This Dance Before" was born.

My parents loved to dance. Anytime there was live music playing they were always the first ones out on the floor. The beginning of our work on the *Dignity* project coincided with my dad starting to do full-time caregiving for my mom, who was suffering with a terminal blood disease. I realized that my subconscious had been at work on a song to honor my parents as they entered, after almost sixty years of marriage, into a new and very different "dance" together.

"We've Never Done This Dance Before," set as a waltz, is a tribute to all of the spouses who have decided that, even given the chance, they "still wouldn't sit this one out."

What a Friend

I knew that we would have to take on the subject of Alzheimer's disease on the *Dignity* project, but unbeknownst to me I would need to look no farther than my friend Corey, who had been my co-writer on "Wildest Ride on Earth" and the producer of both the *More Beautiful* and *Somebody's Daughter* DVDs. We were sitting in his living room one evening when I told him that we were going to be working on a project for caregivers. He then proceeded to tell me a miraculous story.

Corey's grandmother had been in a nursing home suffering from Alzheimer's. Corey visited her often in the evenings. He talked with her, brushed her hair, and sang to her. A few weeks before her death her disease got so bad that she would speak to Corey without realizing it was him. She would tell him all about her grandson (Corey) and how much his singing blessed her. She would ask him if he could stay until her grandson got there so that he could hear him sing. Corey never corrected her.

Toward the end of his grandmother's life, things got really bad. Her feet and hands started turning black, and she couldn't close her mouth anymore. Finally one night when she was in so much pain that tears were steaming down her face, Corey just couldn't stand to watch her suffer any longer.

"I remember having my hand on her cheek," he recalls. He thought, *All I need to do is just gently slide my hand over her mouth and pinch her nostrils shut. Then she could pass and be in heaven.*

He remembers pulling his hand away, appalled at what he had almost done. He realized he was very angry with God. His grandmother's lingering on and on just didn't make any sense to him. She died a few days later.

Three or four months after the funeral, Corey was talking to his mother, and she told him that the night before his grandmother died his aunt had visited the nursing home. This was his grandmother's youngest daughter and the one who had given her the most trouble through the years. She had spent the evening talking to her mom, holding her hand, and letting her know how she loved her. "It was a healing moment," Corey said. "And I would have taken that away from her had I acted, thinking I was wiser than God."

After Corey shared that story with me, we worked together on a song called "You Should Hear Him Sing," based upon the story and the words his grandmother used to say to him. When it came time to produce the song, I deliberately left an open space in the arrangement of the piece so that Corey could sing a hymn a cappella, reenacting the way he used to sing for his grandmother.

I called him and said, "I want everything to go silent for a moment, and then I want you to sing a verse of 'What a Friend We Have in Jesus.'" There was an extended silence on the other end of the line. "What's wrong," I asked?"

"Had I ever told you?" said Corey.

"Told me what?"

"That was my grandmother's favorite song. That was the song I would always sing to her."

I got a chill. "No, you never told me that."

Corey's story and the song he shared on *Dignity* is just one of the many times when I have found myself grateful for the privilege of being able to share such sacred and holy moments through the ministry.

One of the hardest things for caregivers to talk about when caring for an elderly loved one is the fact that, no matter how wonderful a job they do, they cannot change the end of the story. Eventually, the person they are caring for is going to die. Shelly felt that it was critically important that there was a song on the project that would give vent to this pain. I feel like this is the kind of a thing a song can do better than any other form of communication. This is because a song, in a gentle and non-confrontational way, can mirror the experience of the listeners through a story that tells the truth about what they are feeling. God can minister privately in someone's heart as they listen, enabling them to relate to the message without having to talk or be vulnerable to another person. In addition, the music can express those feelings that are simply beyond words.

Because of the timing of this project, I knew this was going to be a song that would be both very easy and terribly difficult to write. It would be easy because the lyrics would be autobiographical. It would be difficult because of the emotion I was feeling.

After ten years of fighting a rare blood disease, my mother's health was beginning to fail.

As I worked on "I'm Gonna Lose You," the challenge was to state something deeply personal in a way that would resonate for others for whom the loss of a loved one was imminent. I wanted to convey, both in the lyric and the music, how bittersweet the situation is. On the one hand, there is fear of what's to come. And on the other hand, there are the kinds of warm memories that bring a smile to one's face. There is the joy of knowing that our loved one will be in heaven. Yet there is also the inevitable grief that comes with their passing. I wanted to create the music so that, even without the lyric, the melody and harmonization alone would capture all of these conflicting emotions.

> God can minister privately in someone's heart as they listen.

My prayer was that once the words were added both the music and the lyric would have more depth, working together to express feelings that otherwise would be almost inexpressible. Fortunately I was able to finish this song in time for it to be part of dad's last months with my mom. And mom was able to hear in the song how deeply we loved her.

Healing for the Healer

Of the many responses we received regarding the caregiver project, the one that really caught my attention was when a woman referred to *Dignity* as a "companion." Whether running errands to pick up medicine, doing loads of laundry, preparing meals, *Dignity* was something she could listen to that made her feel understood, appreciated, and, most importantly, not *alone.*

I believe this is something songs can do for us—become companions for us as we journey down roads that are often difficult to speak about. The songs can speak for us. By telling our story they can make us feel understood and befriended. They can help us cry the tears we need to cry and breathe the deep breaths we need to breathe, and in so doing they help us begin to heal.

But not only do they offer healing for those who listen to them. They can also offer healing to those who write them. Never was this truer than for "When I Couldn't Do It by Myself."

I felt we needed a song written for the project to honor the loving, professional caregivers who step in and serve and graciously care for someone else's loved one as if they were their own family member.

I knew that a friend at my church, Jeff Crossan, had called in professional caregivers toward the end of caring for his father for two years. At first I asked if he would co-write the song with me, but that was not what happened.

Once he started writing, all of the emotions and pain that he had carried and held inside for so long came bubbling to the surface. His words of gratitude and tribute for those who had helped care for his father poured out in a lovely, heartrending tribute that soothed his hurting soul as much as it ministers to those who hear it.

He came up to me at church and apologized for finishing the song on his own. "Once I got started I couldn't stop. Right after Dad passed away people kept saying to me, 'Man, there's going to be a really good song in this.' But I didn't realize how much I needed to write about it until I started working on the song," Jeff said.

I told him there was no need to apologize. I understood perfectly and was glad we had something for the recording that was straight from his heart. The same thing had happened to me when

I wrote "Whole in the Sight of God" many years earlier. The act of writing can be powerfully cathartic, helping the writer to release feelings that have been pent up in a way that creates not only a song but also brings freedom and peace.

I later had the privilege of watching Jeff perform this song at our church. As I looked around the room, I could see the listeners were moved. It was a wonderful moment of healing, both for Jeff and for many in the congregation.

Caregiving is such a complex issue, not only logistically but also emotionally. One person told me that when Mom or Dad moves into your house they don't only bring their physical baggage. "They bring their emotional baggage as well."

Living in such close proximity, old wounds can be reopened. Long buried, unresolved issues can resurface, creating anger and resentment for weary caregivers. Even though they want to serve their loved one, caregivers might still find themselves feeling trapped and unable to express some of their feelings for fear of seeming insensitive or uncaring. And when the kettle boils over and they *do* say something in a heated moment, they often wind up blaming themselves and feeling guilty.

This can be another place where a song can give vent to what needs to be expressed. On *Dignity* that song is called "In the Middle of the Mess." The listeners can identify with what the singer is experiencing and realize that what they're feeling is normal and they don't have to feel ashamed or guilty.

In the song, various scenarios result in the singer saying, "I got so angry with you. I don't know how much more I can take!" Later, almost defeated, the singer says, "Some days I wish this all would just end, and I feel so bad about that."

When I asked Shelly Beach if there were times when she had felt that her life would be easier if the one she was caring for would just die, she said yes. "Sharing the message through a song that this is a normal reaction to a situation that is so emotionally, physically, and financially draining will give a caregiver permission to have grace for him or herself."

We decided to make the song a duet and let God deliver the message of permission to the caregiver:

> *Let it all out*
> *Feel what you feel*
> *Then look at the guilt but make sure that it's real*
> *'Cause it's easy to be too hard on yourself*
> *Give yourself a break and then rest*
> *And trust in My grace*
> *In the middle of the mess*[3]

In those moments when we are too weary or too immersed in a situation to see past our own pain, songs can help us by telling the stories about our messes, our failures, and our deep hurts, helping us to understand what we are feeling and why.

Caregivers or not, we all have those times when life is simply a mess.

In moments like these, we can be thankful for a God who says, "My grace is sufficient for you" (2 Corinthians 12:9).

Songs from Dignity *an be streamed at www.musicforthesoul.org/resources/dignity.*

16

DRINK DEEP

"Music is the language of the soul made audible."
DON AND EMILY SALIERS

When I founded the ministry of Music for the Soul, I gave a lot of thought to what our first music project should be. As I indicated in chapter 7, I thought we would begin with a grief project. It seemed that the most obvious place to begin was with a topic that everyone experiences at some point in his or her life.

This reminds me of a minor miracle that happened during my tenure as a staff writer at Word. Point of Grace was working on the album that would eventually become *Free to Fly*. David Tyson, a Los Angeles-based producer, had been hired to do some songs on the project. My publisher at the time, Shawn McSpadden, called me into his office one afternoon and told me that Tyson was coming to Nashville to do some co-writing and he wanted to set up a writing meeting for the two of us. I asked Shawn if there was anything in particular that Point of Grace was looking for.

"Yes, they need a concert opener," he replied.

I thought it would be a good idea to spend some time preparing for the meeting, so I went home with the idea of coming up with a lyric suitable for a concert opener. At the time I was receiving a daily devotional booklet in the mail called *Our Daily Bread* from Radio Bible Class, a ministry in Grand Rapids, Michigan. Over the years I'd gotten several wonderful song ideas from reading these devotionals in my quiet time. As a result, I saved all of them and kept them on a shelf in my office. I planned to spend some time looking through the booklets to see if maybe I could find an idea that would inspire a lyric that would work as a concert opener.

Once home, I reached up to the shelf, grabbed about twenty or so of the *Our Daily Bread* booklets, and tossed them randomly onto my desk. The booklet on top popped open to a page with a devotion entitled "Begin with Me."

"Sounds like a good concert opener to me," I said out loud to myself. I scooped the booklets up and put them back on the shelf. The search had taken me all of five seconds. I sat down and wrote the lyric that afternoon. Point of Grace recorded the song and performed it to open the Dove Awards telecast the following year.

I can't think of any other time in my life where a song went from the suggestion stage to the completion stage as quickly and neatly as that. It was the exact opposite of what happened with Music for the Soul and our grief project. It was eleven years *after* I first got the idea that we actually sat down to write the songs. In retrospect, as you probably won't be surprised to learn, God's timing was perfect.

Once we had completed the *Dignity* project for caregivers, it seemed logical that a project dealing with grief might be a good follow-up. After all, the song "I'm Gonna Lose You" on the caregiving record sets the stage for the inevitability of loss. Unfortunately, many of those who are caregiving will soon be dealing with the loss of a loved one.

One of the people who had been very supportive of *Dignity* when it first came out was the Reverend Kaye Harvey. At the time she was working as the minister of pastoral care for Brentwood United Methodist Church in Brentwood, Tennessee. She and I had been talking about ways the ministry and her congregation could partner, and she wound up setting up the opportunity for Music for the Soul to debut the *Dignity* CD live in concert in the church's beautiful chapel.

During the time that all of this was coming together, Kaye shared with me a book she had written about her daughter's passing from breast cancer. It was called *God Is Good, Cancer Stinks, God Is with Us.*[1]

As I read Kaye's book, the themes of grief that emerged tugged at my heart. Song ideas began to come quickly.

Because grief is an intimate experience but also one that has to be lived out within a family dynamic, I felt like this was a topic that needed to be handled differently from any that we'd ever done before. I wanted to be able to explore these feelings in depth over a number of days with a small group of people—much like a family would if they were grieving. We had never done a retreat before to write songs for a Music for the Soul project, but I felt that in this case it might be a helpful process.

I called upon my friends Tony Wood and Scott Krippayne, both of whom I had been in a prayer group with for many years. We'd co-written five full albums between 2002 and 2005 and had come to have a special kind of shorthand when working together. I felt the combination of years of praying together, plus the sixty-plus songs we had co-written as a threesome, would give us the ability to go to the deep, vulnerable places we needed to explore if we were going to do the project justice.

I called a long-time ministry friend and supporter Sharalena Miller. The Millers have a beautiful vacation home in the country, and I asked Sharalena if we could stay there for three or four days—in a peaceful setting away from all that might distract us—in order to submerge ourselves in the work. She graciously agreed.

A few weeks later Scott, Tony, and I headed off for a trip unlike most in the country. We all had grief experiences to draw from, but

Scott's was by far the most recent, his mother-in-law having just lost her long battle with cancer.

Once we were settled in, we took turns at the piano and the guitar, building on each other's melody ideas and chord changes. We took time to sit in the silence, contemplating and reworking lyric lines, looking for just the right words to express our feelings. There was much prayer. And even some tears.

I've found through the years that, when spending any length of time tackling dark, heavy issues, it is vitally important to find an opportunity to laugh once in a while. It's one of the ways one can keep from being dragged down into depression after several hours of intense work.

Song ideas began to come quickly.

Well, as everyone knows, the institutional church is well known for its important and commendable tradition of supplying grieving families with meals. Tony, sensing the need for a light moment, provided it when he facetiously suggested we should write a song entitled, "Have I Got a Casserole for You?!" There is no more serious lyricist than Tony Wood, and this well-timed moment of humor allowed us to laugh, take a deep breath, and get back to the difficult work.

By the end of the retreat we had created nine songs, including ones that asked the hardest questions that people face in a time of loss. Why would God allow a loved one to die? What good can come in one's life from living through the loss of a loved one? How does a close relationship survive when two people grieve a loss so differently? And many more.

As was outlined at the beginning of chapter 14, the album format can be very helpful when exploring complicated issues and human emotions. This is especially true when dealing with a topic like grief. That's because a person goes through a wide variety of emotions during the grief process. The process itself is disorderly, with the same questions needing to be revisited and re-resolved a number of times.

Grief therapists have described it to me like being on a spiral staircase where we look at the same pain when it comes around again. The pain looks different because we are in a different place. Support groups, conversations with friends, reading, and sitting with our own thoughts and feelings are all a part of the process. Addressing the ever-changing emotions of grief within the album format allows the songs to work together, over time, to meet the listeners wherever they may happen to be on the grief journey.

> The pain looks different because we are in a different place.

Little did I know when we were creating *Drink Deep* that, all too soon, it would have a deeply personal impact. My mother died just as we were to begin listening to the final mixes for the project. The first person *Drink Deep* ministered to was me.

Since she has been gone, I have felt the emotions expressed in each and every one of the songs on *Drink Deep*, but I have been particularly surprised by the poignant affect of "The Ambush." The song recounts two people, a man in the first verse, and a woman in the second (in the excerpt below), experiencing a sudden, unexpected reminder of their spouse. Of course for me the reminder has been of a parent, but the suddenness of emotion has been no less intense.

> *You'll be going through your closet*
> *Putting summer clothes away*
> *You'll pick up his gray sweater*
> *Catch a scent of aftershave*
> *Then suddenly you're finished*
> *There goes the afternoon*
> *You'll pick up the phone*
> *and call a friend to help you through*
>
> *Through the ambush*
> *That rips your day in two*

Like lightning
A bolt out of the blue
A terrible surprise
Brings tears to your eyes
You thought that you were further past despair
But be prepared
You can never be prepared
For the ambush

You might start hating nights and weekends
and even holidays
It's like walking through a minefield
trying to anticipate, anticipate
the ambush[2]

I've experienced the heartache of this phenomenon multiple times. "The Ambush" has helped prepare me to be able to process the emotions I experience when this occurs without feeling like there is something wrong with me.

A Very Important Function

In the song "No Such Thing as Normal," the vocalist sings about the pain of an irreplaceable loss and how hard it is, especially at the holidays. He would even just prefer to skip Thanksgiving and Christmas.

Where there once was joy and laughter
now my heart is bruised and sore
There's no such thing as normal anymore[3]

As Christians, we want to be the kind of people who are there for others when they are suffering pain because of losing a loved one. However, even the most well meaning of us will be drawn back into our normal routine within a short period of time. A Christian grief counselor once told me that the average church supports a grieving family for about two weeks. A 2009 survey by the Society for Human Resource Management found that, on average, the amount of time employers provide off for bereavement is approximately three days.

While the length of time a person will grieve, and how the grieving process will affect him or her is particular to each individual, it's fair to say that no one is over the death of a loved one in three days. This means there's going to be a prolonged period of time when the one grieving will wonder how everyone else is going on with life as if nothing has changed. "No Such Thing as Normal" acknowledges that something has changed forever.

One listener joked with me that we should make the warning "Do not listen while operating heavy machinery" standard with our recordings. While his comment is humorous, it does speak directly to a very important function that a song can serve.

After the release of our grief project, a woman approached the Music for the Soul table at one of our live events. While looking over our resources, she picked up a copy of *Drink Deep* and asked if she could hear something from the record. I handed her a pair of headphones, and while she was adjusting them, I selected the song "After the Crowds Are Gone" for her to listen to.

> *After the crowds are gone*
> *God will still be near*
> *Sitting with you in your silence*
> *Catching every tear*
> *And He'll meet you there with mercies*
> *that are new at every dawn*
> *After the crowds are gone*[4]

For the first few moments her face was expressionless. But only about thirty seconds into the song, I saw tears spring into her eyes. She pulled the headphones off and with a hasty apology hurried from the room. Several minutes later I approached her and asked if she was OK. She replied, "I didn't realize the pain was that close to the surface."

Many of us walk around every day carrying pain that is close to the surface. Sometimes we suppress it consciously so that we can fulfill whatever responsibilities are expected of us in our work or home life. Other times, we carry it subconsciously, thinking we have dealt with it and moved on.

> We want to be the kind of people who are there for others.

The fact is that most of us carry buried memories and unhealed wounds from our past.

Dr. Doris Sanford taught me that the old axiom "time heals all wounds" is actually incorrect. "Time is neutral. It heals nothing," she said. She went on to explain that until we deal with our unresolved feelings they are exactly that—unresolved.

We live in a culture that moves quickly and all too often moves on *too* quickly—not allowing people the time they need to process painful feelings from grief or other difficult life events. The feelings of hurt that we carry unconsciously need an outlet. Songs can help. When a song elicits the kind of instantaneous response that "After the Crowds Are Gone" did for the woman, it can provide a healthy release for feelings that need to be felt and processed in order for healing to come.

When this happens it can, in fact, feel like an ambush. But while the word *ambush* carries a negative connotation, this actually can be something positive. The tears we shed are a part of the healing process, watering the ground so that the life-giving shoots of a new normal can emerge from the tender soil of our storm-battered hearts.

As Good as Good-bye Gets

Since, as was noted in the previous chapter, music goes to the place in the brain where emotions are processed, it should come as no surprise that songs about grief are able to express those feelings that people have been unable to put into words regarding the death of a loved one.

In his wonderful book *A Grace Disguised,*[5] author Jerry Sittser, who lost three of his family members in a tragic car accident, says, "In the months following the accident I listened to music almost every night." He speaks of "the power music has to touch the deepest places in the human heart" and how "music touched the anguish of my soul and gave me peace."

Sittser's comments affirm what I have experienced over and over again. A song has the power to bring comfort, peace, and the light of hope to the darkest passages in our lives.

Hope is like air. We need it to live as much as we need food and shelter. Author Hal Lindsey took it even further, saying, "Man can live about forty days without food, about three days without water, about eight minutes without air . . . but only for one second without hope." To live without hope is to despair of the future. God knows how much we need it. Scripture says we need not grieve as those who have no hope (see 1 Thessalonians 4:13). Through Jesus Christ, God has given us "a living hope" (1 Peter 1:3).

Since much of *Drink Deep* was necessarily sad, it was very important that the project finish with a hopeful message, reflecting the hope found in the Scriptures, the hope we have in Christ.

Like I said earlier, most of the songs for *Drink Deep* were written on a retreat. As we were preparing for our time away and talking through what themes we felt the recording should include, Tony Wood said, "Well, we already have the song for the ending."

He was referring to "Death Has Been Conquered," a song that John Mandeville and I had written several years earlier for the *Dancing with Angels* project.

It is disarmingly simple. John and I were sitting at his kitchen table in Franklin, Tennessee, when we wrote the song. He was gently strumming his guitar, and the six lines of the lyric came easily. I remember thinking, *This can't be all there is. We need to say more.* But there was nothing more to say.

> *Death has been conquered*
> *The victory won*
> *Christ lives forever in God's daughters and sons*
> *The cross is the entrance*
> *Faith is the key*
> *Death has been conquered for you and for me*[6]

My first reaction to Tony's suggestion was that maybe we should take another run at this theme. I tend to think that newer is better or that there ought to be more.

One of the wonderful things about a song is that it has a life all its own. It can reach out across the miles and be heard in faraway places. Often I have looked at my foreign royalty statement, listing the countries where a song has been heard, and smiled because one of my "children" has gone somewhere I've never been and probably will never go.

But not only can songs reach across geography. They can also reach out across time and speak to generations beyond the life span of the author. And even though a song may be "old," when someone hears a song who has never heard it before, it becomes new again!

Tony was paying me the best compliment a writer can ask for. He felt like the straightforward little song that John and I had written sixteen years earlier deserved the opportunity to speak once again. I thanked him and gratefully agreed that perhaps we should include the song. Ironically, I immediately had the chance to return the favor without even realizing I was doing it!

I said, "While we're at it, there's another song that has already been written that I would like to include. I heard Joel Lindsey sing it several years ago at Write About Jesus. It's called 'As Good as Goodbye Gets.'" The song is a tender, moving tribute to a person who has lived life in a way that has honored Christ.

> With Jesus' saving act on the cross, death has been conquered.

Now anyone who has known Tony Wood for five minutes will tell you that humble is his middle name. He once won the ASCAP* Lyricist of the Year award and didn't bother to tell his own prayer group. But even he, in this moment, had to take credit for what he knew I would find out anyway.

"I co-wrote that song with Joel," Tony said.

Thus, *Drink Deep* was begun with the solid cornerstone of our faith already in place, an assurance that gives us the ultimate hope. With Jesus' saving act on the cross, death has been conquered. And that truly *is* as good as good-bye gets.

Songs from Drink Deep *may be streamed at www.musicforthesoul.org/resources/drink-deep.*

---

* American Society of Authors, Composers, and Publishers (ASCAP) is one of the three royalty collections agencies for songwriters. The other two are BMI and SESAC.

17

BROKEN TO BLESS

"God uses broken things. It takes broken soil to produce a crop,
broken clouds to give rain, broken grain to give bread,
broken bread to give strength. It is the broken alabaster box
that gives forth perfume. It is Peter, weeping bitterly,
who returns to greater power than ever."
VANCE HAVNER

In 2008 I decided it was time for me to write a theme song for the ministry of Music for the Soul. Full of good intentions, I sat down and proceeded to pen a manipulative, heavy-handed, self-conscious, dreadful piece of drivel. I played it for only one other person before deciding it belonged in a drawer, where it safely resides to this day.

Then one afternoon in 2013, I walked into the sanctuary of First Christian Church, a beautiful and historic downtown church in Frankfort, Kentucky. Soft light was coming through the stained-glass windows. The large sanctuary, with its dark wooden pews and deep red carpet, was inviting in its solitude. At the left of the chancel stood a grand piano. I sat down and begin to play with nothing particular in mind.

What poured out over the next couple of hours was "Broken to Bless," a song that I think captures the heart of Music for the Soul better than anything I could have ever tried to do deliberately.

As Christians, we all want to become more and more like Jesus as we grow in faith. Of course, only Jesus is the Christ, so in a sense we are pursuing an unattainable goal. None of us is, or ever can be, perfect.

But here's the thing. At first it may seem counterintuitive, but I believe it is actually in our brokenness and vulnerability that we can be most like Jesus. God used the brokenness of Jesus on the cross to bless us. God can also use our brokenness to be a blessing for others.

Suddenly I could breathe again.

Jesus said He did not come to be served but to serve. Sometimes our most disappointing personal failures can act as bridges helping us to understand and be with someone in their pain. It is then that we are being more like Jesus than we ever could by consciously trying to be holy or righteous.

I remember a time in my early twenties when I was really hurting over something I'd done. I was so upset that I drove over to my friend Adam's apartment and poured out my heart.

I still remember him shaking his head and smiling. Then he said, "When someone is that honest with you, they deserve for you to be honest in return." He then proceeded to tell me the truth about a lie he had told me that I had believed. His willingness in that moment to reveal a secret broken place in his own life was an act of grace. Suddenly I could breathe again.

Our brokenness, shared in the right moment, might be the very thing someone needs to begin to heal, to find peace, to find freedom. And we might find that by sharing our most difficult experiences with others they take on new meaning and purpose.

The songs that come when they are ready are the ones that work the best. I don't think I could've written "Broken to Bless" any earlier in my life than I did. I had to live it first. Life has a way of working us over, making us more receptive to the will of God. Yes, God is the potter and we *are* the clay. But hardened clay cracks. It is only when we become pliable—more responsive to God's prompting—that God's will can have its way with us.

I never expected to create and run a not-for-profit music ministry. As expanded on in earlier chapters, it was only after several years of life experiences—including many disappointments and disillusionments—that I was able to ascertain God's leading. God was very patient with me.

It was only once I stopped straining so hard to get my own way, stopped resisting God's molding, that I was able to find the path of obedience. I believe that path is the source of all true freedom. God has a plan for my life and wants what's best for me: "'For I know the plans I have for you,' declares the LORD, 'plans to prosper you and not to harm you, plans to give you hope and a future'" (Jeremiah 29:11).

Once willing to live in obedience to God, how can I not help but find deeper meaning for my life? How can I not help but be of more service to others? Isn't that where our identity in Christ is most likely to be found? Jesus said of Himself, "The Son of Man did not come to be served, but to serve" (Matthew 20:28). There is such great hope in that—hope for a life that is full of love and rich in mercy and grace.

> *We don't learn humility*
> *from our successes*
> *The failures we go through*
> *teach us the most*
> *I could put on a brave face*
> *act like I'm in control*
> *or point to the One who I trust with my soul*
>
> *Because I've been broken*
> *How deeply I can bless*
> *Compassion's been forged in the fires of duress*

As Jesus did for me
How could I do any less?
I've been broken, broken
broken to bless[1]

On my journey in ministry, I have had the privilege of coming to know many people who are living examples of being broken to bless. These are people who could have given up, and nobody would have blamed them. Their stories are stories of people who have surrendered control and chosen to trust God to bring light out of the darkness:

- Sue Foster, who used the brokenness she experienced through surviving the suicide death of her daughter to become a Christian counselor, blessing others as she helps them heal from their grief.
- Michael Cusick, who used the brokenness of his own sexual addiction to create a ministry called Restoring the Soul, blessing men and couples by helping them to be set free from the bonds of their sexual addiction.
- Stevey Shaw, who survived the brokenness of abuse as a child and cancer as an adult and is now working toward certification as a spiritual director in order to bless those who are seeking God's leading in their lives.

These are only three examples. I could list literally dozens and dozens of inspiring people who I have met personally—people who have taken the ashes in their lives and turned them into something beautiful, people who are living examples of Romans 8:28: "And we know that in all things God works for the good of those who love him, who have been called according to his purpose."

Because of faithful people like these, and the Word of God, I have no doubt whatsoever that it is in our most broken places that the hope of Christ can be found.

The Right Song

Dr. Deforia Lane turned away from a career as an opera singer to become a music therapist working with seriously ill people to help them find new joy and hope.[2] In her book *Music as Medicine*, filled with astonishing accounts of music's effectiveness in working with patients afflicted with a variety of maladies, she refers to something she calls therapy of the soul. "Music and healing are often matters of the human spirit," Dr. Lane says.

I once saw a sign on the outside of a Christian bookstore. It read: BE KIND. EVERYBODY IS HAVING A HARD LIFE.

Sometimes our brokenness is almost invisible. You don't have to have had a tragic accident in your family. You don't have to be seriously ill. Sometimes the stresses and pressures of ordinary life weigh on us in crushing ways that are almost impossible to see for those looking at our lives from the outside.

At times like these we need something that can lift our flagging spirit. We need something that can seep into the cracks and crevices of our broken hearts, a salve that can sooth and console and mend. Music can do this and more. The right song can tell our truth in a way we've never heard or felt it before. The right song can give us the key to a door we thought was locked forever. The right song can bring us alive and remind us who we are. The right song can give our pain meaning . . . even beauty, as the title song of this chapter suggests.

There is almost nothing that can have the immediate impact on our mood that a song can have. Without ingesting any mind-altering substances at all, we can find our emotional landscape completely transformed inside of three minutes.

When we hear the first strains of one of our favorite joyful songs, we can find ourselves singing or dancing involuntarily. Before we know it, we have forgotten whatever was troubling us a moment ago and have been transported into the joy of the song. Without changing our physical location at all, we can find ourselves swiftly transported back in time, a song evoking places and times that carry deep and powerful significance for us.

Everyone needs things in their life that will lift their spirit. An intimate conversation with a good friend can do it. Worship and prayer can do it. A walk in the woods or on the beach can do it. An inspiring story in the form of a good book or a good movie can do it. The laughter of a child can do it. But, whether to process feelings of pain in ways that ultimately bring resolution and peace or to experience joy that can lift us out of the deepest doldrums, there is no doubt that music can make everyone's life a little less hard. And a little more blessed. That, as Dr. Lane suggests, is indeed "therapy for the soul."

It's a Mystery

To paraphrase the brilliant Joni Mitchell, I've "looked" at *songs* from both sides now.* I have looked at songs as a listener, enjoying them as the constant companions of the formative years of my youth. I have looked at them as a professional, with the privilege of having written and having had songs recorded in three consecutive decades.

I've studied them, analyzed them, constructed and deconstructed them, praised them, criticized them, adored them, been infuriated by them, and been transported everywhere from the ridiculous to sublime and the profane to the sacred by them.

---

* "I've looked at clouds from both sides now." "Both Sides Now" words and music by Joni Mitchell, *Clouds* album, 1968.

Still, at the end of the day, songs remain a mystery.

Oh sure, songwriting has rules. It's a craft, a hard-won craft that requires tremendous commitment and a relentless work ethic. But there is more to it than that. An alchemy takes place when it is working that makes the sum greater than its parts. There comes a time when it ceases to be just words and music and becomes something else.

Not every song has it. Even songwriters who have done it for years and had lots of success still can't really explain where the great stuff comes from. First it's not there and then it is.

There is a God piece that is pure gift. Anyone can learn *about* it, but not everyone can learn to *do* it. Yes, I believe one can learn the rules of melody writing; but Paul McCartneys and Stevie Wonders are not born every day of the week, and no amount of rule following will make someone a great melody writer if God didn't put a knack for it into his or her DNA.

> God is the "invisible" co-writer in the room every time a song is being written.

Likewise, one can learn the rules of lyric writing, but Jon Foremans and Carole Kings don't grow on trees either. If God has not granted a person acuity for language, then the peak of that mountain is not likely to be scaled.

Even if God *has* granted that gift, and even if a person works assiduously at it for years, there is no foolproof formula for writing that truly special, world-changing song every time out. If there was, then every songwriter would write an unbroken string of hits and not even the best of the best succeed at that.

The difference between good and great? It's a mystery. But I have a feeling I know who is behind the mystery.

God.

God is the "invisible" co-writer in the room every time a song is being written. God is the invisible artist in the room when a painter lifts the brush to canvas, the invisible director when an actor brings a character to life, the invisible choreographer when a dancer's body becomes poetry in motion. In short, God, the original Creator, is the unseen collaborator in all the forms of creativity that grace our earth.

At the end of the day, I believe there is something sacred in the act of creativity. And I believe when it all comes together in a way that not even the artist can adequately explain it is because God has played a part in the process. You'll hear a lot of writers refer to inspiration. I think inspiration is another word for God's spirit. Inspiration is God whispering to us and speaking through us. Hallelujah!

I believe this is true whether the artist acknowledges God or not. But I'm grateful for the experience of having worked with songwriters and musicians over the years who *do* acknowledge God's participation in the process and who, with humility, find it a wonder and an honor to be able to give birth to songs that touch and change lives.

Music has changed my life. And as I have shared through many of the examples in these pages, I have seen songs impact the lives of countless others, where there was despair bringing hope, where there was fear restoring faith, and where there was bondage offering freedom.

I have felt my spirit soar to the highest heights in response to a piece of music. And I have literally been driven to my knees by a song, feeling the dam break inside of me as a song released a flood of almost unendurable mercy to wash away my guilt.

No other form of communication has touched me as profoundly in both sorrow and joy.

While music is found in many forms in our world and is used in many ways, I believe that music, especially as it is expressed in song, is first and foremost the greatest gift of communication that God has ever given us. Ultimately, I believe God has given us music for the nourishment of our souls and calls us to use that gift to communicate our human experiences in ways that facilitate the celebration of the richness of life and the expression of love to and for one another.

"Broken to Bless" may be streamed at
www.musicforthesoul.org/resources/broken-bless/.

Appendix A

HOW MUSIC AND SONGS CAN BE USED

By Suzanne Foster, MA, LMFT

"Music is God's best gift to man, the only art of heaven given to earth, the only art of earth we take to heaven."
WALTER SAVAGE LANDOR

Music is hardwired to our souls and releases our stories. Songs carry the unique power to unleash healing beyond the ability of words and images alone. Music is the language of celebration, comfort, mourning, joy, worship and praise—of every human emotion.

In the following pages you will find some suggestions for how songs, and more specifically Music for the Soul (MFTS) resources, can be used in church and counseling settings. Traditional music therapy has shown great results in restoring motor function and cognitive function in some patients often with remarkable results. For more on this topic, take a look at the suggested reading list at the end of the appendix.

While not music therapy in the way that the term is currently understood, songs have proven effective in my own practice and for hundreds of colleagues I've spoken to during the past twenty years in helping achieve breakthrough with their clients. I eagerly await the completion of empirical studies that will validate what my experience and the overwhelming tide of anecdotal evidence suggests; namely, that songs can and do make a difference in helping people find healing and resolution around difficult psychological issues.

In addition to the suggestions offered in the following pages, you may find other ways that these materials are helpful to you in your ministry environment or counseling practice. We have heard from many therapists and pastors who have found creative ways to use songs to benefit those whom they serve.

God bless you in your ministry of caring for and offering hope in the name of Jesus Christ.

Suggestions for Using MFTS Resources in a Church Setting

To speak to hurting hearts,
show God's merciful, loving care,
His ability to reconcile,
and the renewing, healing power of Jesus Christ.

- As a take-home piece for someone in your congregation who is working through or struggling with a particular issue and/or for the family and friends of this person as a way to help them understand what their loved one is going through
  - Someone who is grieving, a family that is caregiving, a woman with breast cancer, a man struggling with pornography addiction, a young woman working to overcome an eating disorder, etc.
- To introduce "difficult" sermon topics such as pornography, suicide, or body image
- In pastoral counseling—as an opening in a counseling session when you don't know what to say
- As part of topical multi-media presentations
- As part of original dramatizations
- In Bible study groups
- As a take-home piece for message reinforcement

- In church-sponsored support groups and recovery programs
- In educational settings:
  - Adult Sunday school classes, topical retreats, and workshops
  - Working with teens or young adults—to prompt discussions
- As training tools for staff, lay leaders, and others who minister in your church
- As a gift for visitors and on special holidays:
  - *Psalm 23* as a gift for first-time visitors or as a token of appreciation to Sunday school teachers and lay leaders.
  - *50 Years from Now* as a giveaway to the couples in your church on Valentine's Day.

Suggestions for Using MFTS Resources in a Counseling Setting

To elicit an emotion, break the ice,
overcome denial, soften a resistant heart,
to help process, to reinforce a message

These resources are additional tools in the therapist's toolbox.

- In individual therapy to:
  - Help build trust while establishing the therapist-client relationship
  - Open a discussion
  - Help break down walls of defense and denial
  - Help build a bridge of empathy and understanding between the therapist and client
  - Create a safe place for the client
- In therapy and recovery groups
  - Songs, such as "Free" from *Somebody's Daughter*, can be used as stand-alone pieces when starting a new group to give participants a sense of direction and hope, and something to work toward
- Self-disclosure, when appropriate, has become easier for the professional through the use of these resources.
- In conferences, topical retreats, and workshops

- Use for role playing
- As "homework" to encourage journaling, art, dancing, etc.
- As a take-home piece for continued listening and to help reinforce and retain what is discussed in session
- In conjunction with or instead of reading materials
  - Many clients won't read, but they might listen to music.
  - Other clients may be in too much pain to concentrate on and retain written material but can close their eyes and allow the music to wash over them.

Equipping for Soul Care

While each of the MFTS resources covers a specific issue, we know that healing is not a linear process and is usually very disorganized. With this in mind, we have designed our resources so that each index can function effectively on its own. Though the CDs are designed so that one can listen to them as a complete journey, it may be that the person you are serving will need to listen to one song or one spoken-word piece several times before being ready to move on to a different idea. Many of our songs and spoken-word pieces can be used for a variety of issues and can therefore be used out of the context in which they were originally placed.

Whether it is an issue of finding the right timing or of finding the idea that will most resonate, it is always up to you as the caregiver to prayerfully discern when an individual might best be served by a specific MFTS piece.

Suggestions for Using Individual MFTS Songs

After the Storm—Providing hope for those who are depressed and dealing with the storms and losses of life.

"Binder of the Broken" shows God's love in any situation.

"Where Is the Ground?" is for those who have lost hope and fear the future.

"Not Too Far from Here" reminds listeners that God is present and gives comfort and compassion in the midst of their pain.

Chaos of the Heart—Grieving the loss of a loved one to suicide.

"How Could You?" is for those who have the "why" questions and wonder where God is in their pain.

"Every Single Tear" assures listeners that God sees and cares about their pain and tears, no matter their sorrow.

"Keep Breathing" encourages listeners to keep going and not give up in the face of adversity.

Note: An accompanying digital discussion guide is available.

Fifty Years from Now—For marriages that need strengthening and encouragement.

"Fifty Years from Now." Even the best of marriages experience difficulty. This is a reminder to couples that no matter what they are going through, their marriage vows are sacred. It is also a window onto the potential impact of choosing divorce on their life and the lives of others moving forward.

"I Don't Know You Anymore" is an honest look at how the demands and stresses of everyday life make it difficult to maintain intimacy in a marriage.

"Before God" reminds couples to keep their relationship under God's protection and blessing and honor their commitments.

More Beautiful DVD/CD—For breast cancer survivors and their families.

"More Beautiful" provides spousal support for those facing surgery, disease, and change in appearance.

"Wildest Ride on Earth" is for those times when life feels like a roller coaster.

Note: An accompanying digital discussion guide is available.

Somebody's Daughter DVD/CD—A journey to freedom from pornography.

"Somebody's Daughter" reminds the listener of the divine in all people.

"Is It Me?" From the woman's point of view, this song honestly addresses the pain of being in relationship with someone who is trapped in pornography.

"Into the Light" shares the truth that shining the light of Christ on a problem is the beginning of overcoming the darkness.

"Free" offers hope and release from addiction.

"DVD"— A documentary and music videos to reinforce the message and issues surrounding pornography addiction.

Note: An accompanying printed discussion guide is available.

Tell Me What You See—For those overcoming eating disorders.

"Beautiful Jesus" speaks to anyone with self-image and self-esteem issues.

"To Be Free" is for the person who is dealing with addictive or negative behaviors and longs to be free.

"Time for a Breakdown" is about finding God at the end of our own strength.

"Just the Way that I Am" is for those who need to know that God loves them where they are right now.

Note: An accompanying digital discussion guide is available.

Twenty-Three—Comfort and inspiration for all times and in all situations.

This performance of the Twenty-Third Psalm offers hope, restoration, redemption, peace, and healing and is a reminder of the constant, loving presence of our Lord.

Whole in the Sight of God—For families raising special needs children.

"Whole in the Sight of God" is for anyone who feels that they are not loveable because they are less than perfect.

Dignity—Songs and stories for caregivers.

"Dignity" puts into words what it feels like to be the care receiver and honors the caregiver.

"Returning the Favor" is for the child who is walking the caregiving road alongside a parent.

"Precious Lord, Take My Hand" is for the caregiver who is totally exhausted from the process.

"You Should Hear Him Sing" is to help the family member whose loved one is suffering from Alzheimer's.

"I'm Gonna Lose You" is for the caregiver who is beginning to grieve while still in the caregiving role.

Note: An accompanying printed devotional book with discussion guide questions is available.

Drink Deep—For those who are grieving.

"No" is for persons who are in denial about their loss.

"Don't Feel Much like Prayer Today" is for the person whose faith is challenged or whose prayer life is affected in the wake of a loss.

"Differently" is to help someone when the grieving process is causing difficulties in other close relationships.

"Good" is to help grieving persons looking for meaning in the passing of their loved one.

"Death Has Been Conquered" is to reassure those who are grieving that Christ has the final say and that their loved one is in heaven.

Broken to Bless—God's love meeting us in difficult places.

"Innocent Child" is to help survivors of child sexual abuse know that the abuse was not their fault.

"Child of Mine" is to let listeners know that they don't have to earn God's love.

"Wounded Angel" is to let those who have made mistakes know that God still sees them as His precious child.

"The Apology" is to help men, in particular, understand how a culture of objectification damages a person. It is also to "stand in the gap" for women who have never heard "I'm sorry" from those who wounded them.

Single Songs

"Crooked Road" is for the person who is living with a chronic medical condition.

"Prayer for You" is for military members and their families separated by deployment.

"Days of Hope" is to encourage those serving the homeless.

"Child of God" is to educate churches about the issue of sex trafficking and to encourage sex-trafficked persons to know that God loves them.

"It Doesn't Feel like Christmas This Year" acknowledges the pain of going through the first round of family holidays after the passing of a loved one.

Appendix B

CHAPTER QUESTIONS TO PONDER AND DISCUSS

Chapter 1, Road to a Prayer

1. What instrument did you learn—or want to learn—as a child?

2. Can you remember a music teacher, or any other teacher, who really challenged you? What did you learn from that experience?

3. Is there a decision you made out of fear that later made you feel ashamed before God? How did that change you?

4. Have you ever prayed a prayer in your life that you felt was a turning point? How did God answer?

Chapter 2, The Soundtrack of Our Lives

1. Can you name a song that has told a part of your story? How did that affirm your experience?

2. At what types of live gatherings have you seen a song change or set the tone for the event? Why do you think that is?

3. Can you think of a time when a song has created a deeper level of understanding by taking something you have always known

in your head and putting it into your heart? What kind of a difference has that made?

4. What gifts and talents has God given you to share with our hurting world? Ask close friends to tell you what gifts *they* see in you.

Chapter 3, A Path of God's Design

1. Do you have a mission statement for your life? If so, what is it? If not, what might your mission statement be?

2. Has there been a time when a song has changed your thinking about something? In what way?

3. Do you feel like God has ever "winked" at you? Has there been a season of life when you felt as if you experienced God's hand in real time? How did that change the way you see God?

4. A familiar passage of Scripture can sometimes mean something different to us at different times in our life. Can you name a song that has taken on a different meaning for you in different seasons? Explain how.

Chapter 4, Not Too Far from Here

1. In what ways is Jesus "not too far from here" in your life? In your community?

2. Has there been a time when you wanted to pray and felt you had no words? What are some songs that have been prayers for you?

3. Is there some area of your life where you feel like you have been waiting for permission? Whose permission are you waiting for?

4. Can you describe a "coincidence" you have experienced that in retrospect was clearly God's leading hand in your life?

Chapter 5, Circle of Friends

1. What are some of the pebbles you have thrown into the pond? How have you seen the ripples come back to you?

2. Think of a time you made a "leap of faith." What did putting on the crash helmet teach you about trusting God?

3. Has God answered a prayer you prayed or honored a commitment you made to Him even when you had forgotten about it? What does that say about God's faithfulness?

4. Stop and think about the circle of friends God has created in your own life. Who are some of the people whose presence in your life has made such an impact on you that they have a hand in every life you touch?

Chapter 6, Why a Song?

1. What examples of rhythm, melody, and harmony can you find in nature? In man-made society?

2. God has given us many different forms of creative expression. Can you identify the different ways of "knowing" that most resonate with you?

3. Can you think of a time when a song has melted your "wall of defense"? Why do you think it was able to do that?

4. What is a song worth to you, and how do you define its value?

Chapter 7, More Beautiful

1. Beverly talked about the song "More Beautiful" "lifting a great weight" off her shoulders. Can you describe a time when you have experienced a physical response to a song?

2. Have you ever heard someone talk about a song and realized it meant something completely different to you? How is it that the same song can speak differently to different people?

3. Why do you think songs can awaken unresolved feelings?

4. Is there a painful story in your life that God has been able to use to bless someone else? In what way did that change how you felt about what you had been through?

Chapter 8, *Whole in the Sight of God*

1. Parents who pray for their children to be healed will experience vastly different outcomes from family to family. Do you have a personal philosophy about how God answers prayer?

2. Can you think of a time God used your own creativity to heal a wounded place in you? What happened?

3. Scott was moved to tears singing "Whole in the Sight of God." Why do you think songs make us cry?

4. Has there been a song that made you feel "like somebody understands"? What did that mean to you?

Chapter 9, *Horizontal Worship*

1. The next time you are part of a praise and worship service, pay careful attention to the lyrics. Would they resonate with someone who isn't a Christian? Why or why not?

2. Take a look at a hymnal. Can you identify which of the old classic hymns are vertical and which are horizontal? Are some both?

3. What are some of the songs that have made you feel the closest to God? Can you explain why?

4. Can you name one song that you feel more accurately than any other captures your faith story? If so, what is it?

Chapter 10, *Comfort in the Chaos*

1. If you were going to pitch a tent and camp out with a song theme, what would it be?

2. Has there ever been a time when you felt that a song did not "ring true" with regard to an issue where you had life experience? How did that make you feel?

3. Has God ever used a song to help you vent your anger or some other emotion? Describe the experience.

4. How is a song like a conversation?

Chapter 11, Somebody's Daughter

1. Do you have a secret struggle? Is there a song out there that speaks what you have yet to feel you can name?

2. Has there been a time when you heard a song and thought, *Well, I guess I'm not crazy after all?* Is there something about hearing that kind of message in song form that makes it especially affirming?

3. God took away Clay's voice to get his attention. In what ways, subtle and not so subtle, has God gotten your attention?

4. What is the song in your heart?

Chapter 12, Binder of the Broken

1. Can you think of times when songs have evoked powerful memories of "place" for you? Was it the lyric or the music that caused that to happen?

2. Try singing a song you normally sing up-tempo in a slower, quieter rendition. How does it change the way the song makes you feel? How does it change the meaning of the words?

3. Why do you think different regions of the country are drawn to different musical styles and identities?

4. What does it mean to you that Jesus is the "Binder of the Broken"?

Chapter 13, Tell Me What You See

1. Do you think music videos change how you experience a song? How?

2. To what extent do you think the music industry is responsible for our hyper-sexualized culture? How, if at all, do you think Christians should respond?

3. Can you think of a time a song has helped you broach a conversation topic that was previously "off limits"? Why do you think a song can make a difficult conversation easier?

4. Think about the musical setting of a song that has had an emotional impact on you? What part of that impact was a result of the music? What part of that impact was a result of the lyric?

Chapter 14, Just One Song

1. Which "moment in the river" of your life has been most worthy of a song? Can you name an existing song that captures it?

2. What do you think God has put into music that makes it able to transcend language barriers?

3. Why do you think other people see opportunities for us that we can't see for ourselves? What does this say about how God has created us for community?

4. What is going on in our hearts when God uses a song to free us of some burden that we have been carrying?

Chapter 15, A Companion on the Journey

1. What are some of the ways we can give dignity to the people in our lives?

2. Describe a circumstance or a time when a song has been a companion for you?

3. Can you relate to the feelings Jeff experienced when writing about his father's passing? Why do you think journaling—or writing poetry, stories, and songs—can be so cathartic?

4. Has God ever used a song to bring clarity to something you were having trouble sorting out in your mind? What was it about the song that made things click?

Chapter 16, Drink Deep

1. Is there a time when you have been "ambushed" by a song? When and where did that happen?

2. Has a song every unearthed pain for you that was closer to the surface than you had realized?

3. Are there songs that you turn to when you need to feel God's peace? What are they?

4. Can you think of a simple song that has moved you in a profound way? What about it speaks to you?

Chapter 17, Broken to Bless

1. How does wanting to grow to be more like Christ affect your willingness to be broken for others?

2. Can you describe a time when you felt as if a song has lifted your flagging spirit?

3. What do you think explains the mystery behind the power of songs?

4. Where do you see God's "invisible" hand in the story of your own life?

Notes for Discussion

Notes for Discussion

_____

_____

_____

_____

_____

_____

_____

_____

_____

_____

_____

_____

_____

_____

_____

_____

**Notes for
Discussion**

_____

_____

_____

_____

_____

_____

_____

_____

_____

_____

_____

_____

_____

_____

_____

_____

Notes for Discussion

Appendix C

SUGGESTED READING

This Is Your Brain on Music: The Science of a Human Obsession
 by Daniel J. Levitin

Musicophilia: Tales of Music and the Brain
 by Oliver Sacks

A Song to Sing, a Life to Live
 by Don Saliers and Emily Saliers

Music, the Brain, and Ecstasy: How Music Captures Our Imagination
 by Robert Jourdain

The Power of Music: Pioneering Discoveries in the New Science of Song
 by Elena Mannes

The Healing Power of Sound: Recovery from Life-Threatening Illness Using Sound, Voice, and Music
 by Mitchell L. Gaynor, MD

An Introduction to Music Therapy Theory and Practice (Third Edition)
 by William B. Davis, Kate E. Gfeller, and Michael H. Thaut

ADDITIONAL EXAMPLES OF USING MUSIC TO HEAL

Mercy Music

Mercy music is equipping "musicianaries" to "carry the healing power of music to suffering people all over the world."

http://www.mercymusic.org/about-us/musicianaries

Prodigal Song Ministries

Jim Robinson's testimony is one of overcoming addiction to drugs and alcohol. This ministry uses songs and other resources to offer hope for those dealing with addiction and recovery.

http://www.prodigalsong.com

JoySong Ministries

The nonprofit JoySong Ministries brings the healing power of meditative harp music to the bedsides of people in private homes and medical facilities, to mitigate pain and stress and to support families.

http://www.joysongministries.org

Conducting Hope

A documentary film about a men's choir in a Lansing, Kansas, correctional facility and the transformative effect it is having on the participants.

http://edu.passionriver.com/conducting-hope.html

Music Bridges

Founded by Alan Roy Scott, this organization unites people and cultures around the world through music.

http://www.musicbridges.com

Naomi Feil/Validation Therapy

Naomi Feil demonstrates the power of music to create connection with a virtually nonverbal Alzheimer's patient.

https://www.youtube.com/watch?v=CrZXz10FcVM

MusiCorps

Founded by Arthur Bloom, MusiCorps helps wounded warriors play music and recover their lives.

http://www.musicorps.net/Home.html

Music for Healing and Transition Program, Inc.

This organization certifies musicians to provide live therapeutic music, which creates healing environments for the ill and/or dying and all who may benefit.

http://www.mhtp.org

Operation Song

Songwriting as therapy for the military community, Operation Song was founded by award-winning songwriter Bob Regan.

http://www.operationsong.com

The Music Heals Project

This project grew out of Dr. Christopher Duma's Foundation for Neuroscience, Stroke, and Recovery, raising awareness for the healing power of music for Parkinson's, Alzheimer's, and stroke patients.

http://www.music-heals.com

Healing Music Enterprises

Dr. Alice Cash focuses her work on music's effectiveness in medical settings.

http://www.healingmusicenterprises.com

MercySong

A family-based ministry loyal to the teachings of the Catholic Church, MercySong staff are dedicated to bringing healing through their music, writings, and teachings.

http://www.mercysong.com

Moses' Song

According to its website, Moses' Song is a ministry with a mission to deliver hope, strength, and courage through music and testimony.

http://www.mosessong.org

Christ Song Ministry

This is a prison ministry that uses music to soften the hearts of the inmates, offering them a new hope in Christ.

http://www.christsongministry.org

THANK YOU

"Thank You" sections always scare me. On one of our projects the only person I forgot to thank was the man who gave the largest donation toward the production. No matter how many times you pour over the list, you are bound to forget someone.

So, let me begin by asking forgiveness. If I should have thanked or acknowledged you and your name doesn't appear anywhere in these pages, please know you're in good company!

The fact of the matter is one of the many things I've learned doing ministry is it's a community activity! No matter how much life I might have left, it wouldn't be enough to thank all of the people who have given their time, their money, their talent, their wisdom, their encouragement, and their prayers to make Music for the Soul happen. So, if you fall into one of the categories mentioned above, *thank you*!

You are part of the story, and for that I am grateful.

A special thank you to all the musicians, singers, sound engineers, video technicians, and art designers who have helped create the Music for the Soul catalog and make our projects sound and look so good. Let's do it again!

About the Author

Steve Siler is a songwriter and the founder of Music for the Soul (www.musicforthesoul.org), an award-winning ministry that uses songs and stories to bring the compassion and healing love of Jesus to people struggling with some of life's most difficult challenges.

Siler is a Dove Award-winning songwriter with more than five hundred recorded songs to his credit. He and his wife Meredith have been married for thirty-two years and have two grown children. This is his second book.

ENDNOTES

Chapter One

1. "Forgotten Eyes" © 1985 Lynne McCleery Music

Chapter Two

1. Daniel J. Levitin, *This Is Your Brain on Music* (New York: Dutton, 2006), 250.

2. Karl Paulnack, Welcome address to freshman parents at Boston Conservatory, 2004; Paulnack is a pianist and the director of the Music Division at Boston Conservatory.

3. "Innocent Child," words and music by Steve Siler, © 1990 Fifty States Music, ASCAP (administered by ClearBox Rights, LLC).

Chapter Three

1. As of this writing, the quilt has more than 94,000 names on it and weighs more than fifty-four tons; www.aidsquilt.org.

2. "We're All in This Together," words and music by Steve Siler, © 1991 Lynne McCleery Music, ASCAP.

Chapter Four

1. "Not Too Far from Here," words and music by Ty Lacy and Steve Siler, © 1994 Shepherd's Fold BMI / Ariose, ASCAP (administered by Capitol CMG Publishing).

2. Ibid.

3. Kim Boyce Koreiba is now a Christian counselor, speaker, and author. In 2015, BroadStreet Publishing Group released her book *Not Too Far from Here: Moving from Hurt to Hope.*

4. "I Will Follow Christ," words and music by Clay Crosse and Steve Siler, © 1999 Anything for the Kids / Word Music / Fifty States Music, ASCAP (administered by the Bicycle Music Publishing Company).

5. They are now available at www.musicforthesoul.org as *Music for the Little Soul.*

6. www.douglasshaw.com

Chapter Five

1. http://abcnews.go.com/blogs/headlines/2013/12/starbucks-customers-break-1000-in-pay-it-forward-record/

2. "One Million Reasons," words and music by Aaron Benward, Ty Lacy, and Steve Siler, © 1993 Capitol Christian Music Group. Recorded by Aaron Jeoffrey on Starsong Records.

3. www.writeaboutjesus.com

4. Annie Dillard, *Teaching a Stone to Talk* (New York: Harper & Row, 1982).

5. "Circle of Friends," words and music by Douglas McKelvey and Steve Siler, © 1998 River Oaks Music Publishing Co / Alright Bug Music (administered by Capitol CMG Music) / Magnolia Hill Music (administered by The Bicycle Music Company) ASCAP.

6. I remember this statistic from a California study that was shared with me back in the days before the Internet. Also,

unfortunately, it was before I realized years later I would want to be able to reference it by name. It made such an impression on me because at the time I had just begun working on *I Can't Talk about It.*

Chapter Six

1. As observed in the documentary film *The Music Instinct,* produced by Elena Mannes, 2009.

2. Dr. Sheila Woodward is chair of Music and associate professor of Music Education at Eastern Washington University.

3. *The Music Instinct* documentary

4. I first met Dan when he was senior pastor at Vine Street Christian Church in Nashville, TN. He is the author of *Living with Loss* and *Lose, Love, Live: The Spiritual Gifts of Loss and Change.*

5. Dr. Oliver Sacks, "When Music Heals," *Parade* magazine, March 31, 2002.

6. Daniel Levitin, *This Is Your Brain on Music* (New York: Dutton, 2006), 261. For in-depth discussion of which regions of the brain are involved in processing music and in what order they are engaged, read Levitin's award-winning book.

7. Don and Emily Saliers, *A Song to Sing, A Life to Live* (San Francisco: Jossey-Bass, 2005), 36.

8. Levitin, *This Is Your Brain on Music,* 261.

9. Saliers, *A Song to Sing, A Life to Live,* 43–44.

10. Robert Jourdain, *Music, the Brain, and Ecstasy: How Music Captures Our Imagination* (William Morrow and Company, Inc., 1997), 293.

11. Ibid.

12. M. J. Tramo, "Biology and Music: Enhanced: Music of the Hemispheres," *Science* 291, no. 5501 (2001): 54–56.

13. William J. Cromie, "Music on the Brain," © 2002 *Harvard University Gazette,* archives.

14. Subjective emotional self-experience is stored in the right hemisphere. Marion Solomon and Daniel J. Siegel, eds., *Healing Trauma: Attachment, Mind, Body and Brain* (New York: W. W. Norton & Company, 2003), 15.

15. From the documentary *The Music Instinct: Science and Song.*

16. www.zlab.mcgill.ca/home.php

17. Sari Harrar, "Sing Two Songs and Call Me in the Morning," www.oprah.com/health/Music-Therapy-The-Healing-Power-of-Song.

Chapter Seven

1. "More Beautiful," words and music by Steve Siler, © 2002 Word Music, Inc. / Fifty States Music ASCAP.

2. "Wildest Ride on Earth," words and music by Corey Niemchick and Steve Siler, © 2006 Storytelling Pictures Music and Silerland Music (administered by ClearBox Rights, LLC) ASCAP.

Chapter Eight

1. "Whole in the Sight of God," words and music by Steve Siler, © 2004 Silerland Music (administered by ClearBox Rights, LLC) ASCAP.

2. www.phillipkeveren.com

3. "Crooked Road," words and music by Christopher Bailey and Steve Siler, © 2010 Silerland Music / Ninety Forty Ten Music (administered by ClearBox Rights, LLC), ASCAP.

Chapter Nine

1. Claude King, *The Call to Follow Christ: 6 Disciplines for New & Growing Believers* (Nashville, TN: LifeWay Christian Resources, 2006).

2. "I Choose Grace," words and music by Scott Krippayne, Steve Siler, and Tony Wood, © 2004 Chips & Salsa Songs, New Spring Music Publishing, Fifty States Music/Word Music Inc., ASCAP.

Chapter Ten

1. "Chaos of the Heart," words and music by Steve Siler and Tony Wood, © 2003 Silerland Music (administered by ClearBox Rights, LLC), Row J Seat 9 Songs, and New Spring Music Publishing, ASCAP.

2. David B. Biebel and Suzanne L. Foster, *Finding Your Way after the Suicide of Someone You Love* (Grand Rapids: Zondervan, 2005).

3. "How Could You?," words and music by John Mandeville and Steve Siler, © 1997 Magnolia Hill Music (administered by The Bicycle Music Corporation), ASCAP / Lifestyle of Worship Music BM!

Chapter Eleven

1. "Somebody's Daughter," words and music by John Mandeville and Steve Siler, © 2005 Lifestyle of Worship Music BMI / Silerland Music (administered by ClearBox Rights, LLC), ASCAP.

2. http://www.shessomebodysdaughter.com/get-the-facts -about-pornography

3. "Is It Me?," words and music by John Mandeville and Steve Siler, © 2005 Lifestyle of Worship Music BMI / Silerland Music (administered by ClearBox Rights, LLC), ASCAP.

4. "All of Me," words and music by Kent Hooper, Scott Krippayne, and Steve Siler, © 2003 Word Music Inc., ASCAP.

5. www.holyhomes.org

6. Pastors, Christian counselors, and ministry leaders worldwide have endorsed this multi-award-winning DVD. It comes with an interactive discussion guide written by Michael Cusick for use with the DVD and CD. www.musicforthesoul.org/resources/somebodys-daughter

7. http://www.socioaffectiveneuroscipsychol.net/index.php/snp/article/view/20767

8. Visit www.shessomebodysdaughter.com for more information.

Chapter Twelve

1. www.jamestealy.com and www.sarabethgo.com

2. "Permanent," words and music by James Tealy, © 2005 Universal Music Publishing Group / Cumberland Belle Music (administered by UMPG).

Chapter Thirteen

1. Nicole Barager, November 24, 2014, https://prezi.com/luluw1yf8skq/adverstisments-and-body-image/

2. www.drlindamintle.com

3. www.drgregoryjantz.com

4. "Beautiful Jesus," words and music by Sara Beth Geoghegan, © 2007 Universal Music Publishing Group / Cumberland Belle Music (administered by UMPG).

5. www.findingbalance.com

6. "The Cost," words and music by Missi Hale and Steve Siler, © 2007 Lissabug Music Publishing / Silerland Music (administered by ClearBox Rights, LLC), ASCAP.

7. "Tell Me What You See," words and music by Allie Lapointe and Sara Beth Geoghegan, © 2007 Paper Princess Music / Story City Music BMI.

Chapter Fourteen

1. "Child of God," words and music by Steve Siler, © 2009 Silerland Music (administered by ClearBox Rights, LLC), ASCAP.

2. Shelly Beach and Wanda Sanchez, *Love Letters from the Edge: Meditations for Those Struggling with Brokenness, Trauma, and the Pain of Life* (Grand Rapids: Kregel Publications, 2014).

3. "Prayer for You," words and music by Scott Krippayne, Tony Wood, and Steve Siler, © 2003 Chips and Salsa Songs / New Spring Music Publishing / Silerland Music (administered by Clear Box Rights, LLC), ASCAP.

4. "Heroes Unsung," words and music by Steve Siler, © 2002 Word Music / Fifty States Music, ASCAP.

Chapter Fifteen

1. http://someonecaresonline.com/Movie/Movie.html

2. "Dignity," words and music by Steve Siler, © 2011 Silerland Music (administered by Clear Box Rights, LLC), ASCAP.

3. "In the Middle of the Mess," words and music by Steve Siler and Tony Wood, © 2011 Silerland Music (administered by ClearBox Rights, LLC) / Sony ATV / Songs from Exit 71, ASCAP.

Chapter Sixteen

1. For information about this book, contact kharveysteelers@gmail.com.

2. "The Ambush," words and music by Scott Krippayne, Steve Siler, and Tony Wood, © 2013 Pirk Music, Silerland Music (administered by ClearBox Rights, LLC), ASCAP.

3. "No Such Thing as Normal," words and music by Scott Krippayne, Steve Siler, and Tony Wood, © 2013 Pirk Music, Silerland Music (administered by ClearBox Rights, LLC), ASCAP.

4. "After the Crowds Are Gone," words and music by Scott Krippayne, Steve Siler, and Tony Wood, © 2013 Pirk Music, Silerland Music (administered by ClearBox Rights, LLC), ASCAP.

5. Jerry Sittser, *A Grace Disguised: How the Soul Grows through Loss* (Grand Rapids: Zondervan, 2004).

6. "Death Has Been Conquered," © 1997 Great Dominion Music BMI / Bicycle Music Publishing Company, ASCAP.

Chapter Seventeen

1. "Broken to Bless," © 2013 words and music by Steve Siler Silerland Music (administered by ClearBox Rights, LLC), ASCAP.

2. http://www.musicasmedicine.com